WOODSTOVE COOKERY

At Home on the Range

Jane Cooper

A Storey Publishing Book

Storey Publishing
Pownal, Vermont 05261

To my parents

ACKNOWLEDGMENTS

To begin, I want to thank Walter Goodridge for making this book possible, and my husband, Philip Angell, for his encouragement and editorial assistance. For technical help, I thank Allen Hill, Neal Harrington, Good Time Stove Co., and Lorenzo Morency, all expert stove repairers. And thanks to Jim Patenau, fire chief of our Randolph Center Volunteer Fire Department, who was patient enough to endure my endless questions.

Further appreciation is extended to Shirley Sweedman, Elizabeth Jenkins, Gwen Robinson, Barbara MacCarthy, Perry Wilder, Audrey Lyle, Gladys and Marshall Dimock, and Pat Scheindel, all of whom offered me their time and experience.

And finally, special thanks to my editors, Roger Griffith and Mary Twitchell, for all their help, good humor, and patience.

JANE COOPER

Copyright © 1977 by Storey Communications, Inc.

Storey Publishing books are available for special premium and promotional uses and for customized editions. For further information, please call the Custom Publishing Department at 1-800-793-9396.

Printed in the United States by Capital City Press
20   19   18   17

Library of Congress Cataloging in Publication Data
Cooper, Jane 1946-
  Woodstove Cookery.

  Bibliography: p.
  Includes index.
  1. Stoves, Wood. 2. Cookery. 1. Title.
TX657.S9C66   641.5'8   77-10640
ISBN 0-88266-109-4
ISBN 0-88266-108-6 pbk.

CONTENTS

RECIPES

MAIN DISHES: TOP-OF-THE-STOVE, WOK, AND BAKED

106

CHEESE AND EGGS

125

BROILING AND ROASTING 133

ACCOMPANIMENTS 140

BREADS 147

DESARTS

CAKES

COOKIES

PIES

PUDDINGS AND CUSTARDS

DAIRY

INTRODUCTION

To many people, the use of a wood or coal burning stove may be a questionable step backwards. But when the wood cookstove was first marketed in America, somewhere around 1830, it appeared as the "first major revolution in cooking since the discovery of fire."* Before then, women had cooked in big open hearths and built-in brick ovens. Cooking was often a smoky affair, the kitchen drafty, and there was always the hazard of dragging your skirt through the flames. And so it seems odd that not everybody greeted this revolutionizing wonder with enthusiasm. Harriet Beecher Stowe asked:

> Would our Revolutionary fathers have gone barefooted and bleeding over snow to defend airtight stoves and cooking ranges? I trow not. It was the memory of the great open kitchen fire, its roaring, hilarious voice of invitation, its dancing tongue of flames, that called them through the snows of that dreadful winter.

But many others, however, must have been grateful, for by 1847, the cookstove was in full commercial production.

In the past century, technology has accelerated at a dizzying rate. Scores of machines have replaced the working and thinking of people—and do them better. These advances have freed us from countless laborsome tasks, creating time for more satisfying jobs. But some tasks, though they take more effort, offer greater rewards when done the old-fashioned way. That's how an increasing number of cooks view the wood cookstove. Compared to the operation of its successors, some of which are programmed to de-frost, simmer, broil, and

---

*Kathleen Ann Smallzried, *The Everlasting Pleasure*, Appleton-Century-Crofts, 1956.

1

bake—all in a matter of minutes—wood stove cooking is primitive, demanding much more skill and sensitivity from its operator. Many agree there is greater satisfaction in distinguishing between different woods and the kind of fire each produces, rather than between which button needs to be pushed for what. You are as much responsible for the final product as the stove; rather than being your slave, it's a partner. You learn to cook together.

If you don't already own a wood range, some consideration should be given to what you might expect. Foremost, expect versatility. The stove's surface will provide any kind of heat, from blazing-hot to soothing-to-the-touch, accommodating any kind of frying, simmering or warming, be it food or wet socks. Warming ovens and water reservoirs perform numerous jobs, and some wood stoves are even capable of heating the domestic water supply.

Also, expect flavor. Foods can cook for hours, allowing time for the different ingredients to mingle and harmonize, a service the more frugal-minded might be reluctant to utilize on a stove powered by electricity or gas.

As well as fulfilling a functional role, a wood cookstove also appeals to the senses. Well-polished and clean, it is a pleasure to behold. The feel of its heat is soothing and steady, and the expanding metal ticks with contentment. The aromas from the burning wood and cooking food enrich the air, and citrus peels or cloves, scattered in the back, release a rewarding fragrance.

But a wood stove has its drawbacks. You will need fuel, and if you're doing it yourself, that means felling the tree, bucking to length, splitting and seasoning. Hauling wood into the house

---

"Cooking on a wood stove changes your timing. It's a different rhythm. You start the fire, put on a pan, and cut your onions. By the time they're cut, the stove is hot enough to start sautéeing. Between every cooking juncture, check to see if you need more wood. You have to adjust to the rhythm of the stove rather than the stove conforming to you."

Victoria Weber, Bethel, VT

is not only cumbersome but dirty. And coal, though neater to handle, is no hygienist's dream. The actual cooking of the food is often as demanding as its preparation. You must have patience while the fire starts and the stove heats, and you must be willing to tend the fire for the duration of the cooking.

And because it contains burning fuel, a wood stove deserves the most careful attention. It must be cautiously installed and properly maintained. The risks involved, with what Dickens called "the Red Hot Tyrant," are potentially greater than with other kitchen stoves, but if anticipated and planned for, there need be no worry.

A kitchen range may not be for everyone. It requires more work, time, attention, and patience than a "turn-on" stove; but for those of you who are willing to accept the demands of wood cookstoves, the versatility, delicious meals, warmth and beauty more than compensate.

If you're inexperienced—whether you already own a stove or not—I must ask you to read this book more as a guide than a manual. Although I have used a wood stove for several years and have spoken with many others more experienced than I, my principal finding is that each cook develops his or her own unique techniques. Wood stove cooking methods are as diverse as the stoves and their owners, and so I believe there is no right way, only, in time, your way.

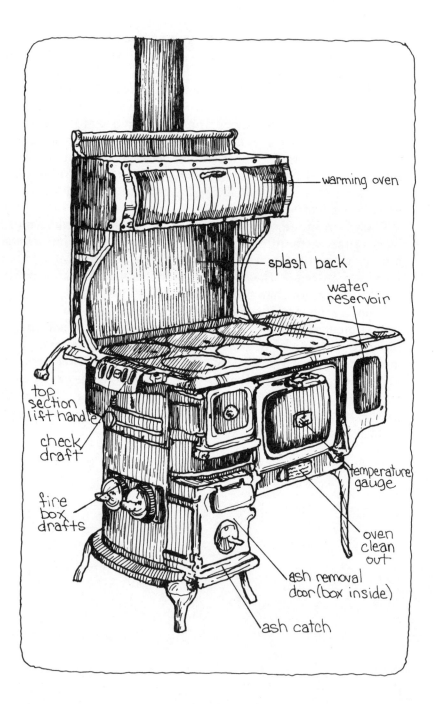

warming oven

splash back

water reservoir

top section lift handle

check draft

fire box drafts

temperature gauge

oven clean out

ash removal door (box inside)

ash catch

PARTS OF THE STOVE

Although there are many different makes and models of wood cookstoves, the various parts and their locations are basically the same. You will have to determine the identification and placement of the parts of your own stove from the illustration and explanation below.

The area where fuel is consumed and heat is produced is called the *firebox*. This is a trough-like compartment, beneath the far left (or sometimes right) cooking lids, where wood or coal is fed and burned. It is reached by either removing the lids, opening the *firebox door* or opening a hinged section of the cooking surface. The material forming the firebox walls is called the *firebox liner*. In wood-burning stoves, it is cast-iron; in coal-burning stoves, it's *firebrick*. Because coal burns much hotter than wood, it needs a more resistant and durable liner.

Forming the base of the firebox is the *grate*. This is what supports the fuel and allows the ashes to fall below. Coal grates are the "shaker type" (Dock-ash, Triangular, and Duplex are a few of the different ones). They are usually made of two, movable, perforated metal halves which, when the *grate bolt* is turned with a special crank, separate and tip back or rotate the halves. This clears the grate of ashes and clinkers (pieces of unburned coal residue), a necessary maneuver for proper coal burning. The sliding wood grate, when in the closed position, holds the wood ash, an essential part of good wood burning. When the grate is opened, the ashes fall into the firebox below. Wood also can be burned on the shaker type grate (the dock-ash grate is designed on one side to hold coal, the other side wood), but also works efficiently on a solid piece "poker type" grate. This grate has narrow openings, either circular or ribbed, which are cleared of ashes with a fire poker. The larger openings on coal grates, necessary for the clinkers to fall through,

5

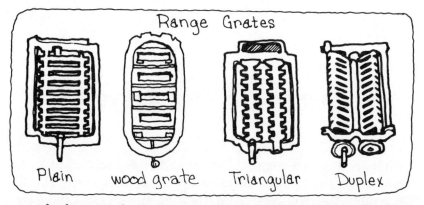

Range Grates

Plain   wood grate   Triangular   Duplex

may feed too much air to a wood fire, making the flames harder to control; also, the wood coals, so vital for holding the heat, easily may be lost.

And most logically, the *ashbox,* into which the ashes and clinkers spill, is directly beneath the grate. This is either a removable box which is pulled out to be emptied, or an integral compartment of the stove which is cleaned by spooning or shoveling out the ashes. The box is located on the front of the stove behind the *ash removal door;* the compartment is reached from the side or the front.

Below the firebox, either on the front or side of the stove, is the *draft.* This can take the shape of a metal plate which slides back and forth exposing a horizontal series of holes, or it can be a metal circle, which when moved around, exposes a circle of holes. Both systems lead beneath the grate, thus controlling the amount of air feeding the bed of burning fuel and, in part, determining the heat of the fire. The more the holes are exposed, the hotter the fire will burn.

Above the firebox on the upper left (or right) side is the *check draft.* This is also a sliding metal plate which exposes a horizontal series of holes. In the open position, it admits room temperature air over the burning fuel which so cools the rising gases that they cannot reach combustion temperature. This, then, "checks," or holds down the fire.

On top of the stove, usually located to the right of the *stovepipe collar*—the projection over which the stovepipe fits—is the *oven damper.* This lever, which moves up and down, back and forth, or side to side (it may also read Bake-Kindle),

controls a metal plate at the base of the stovepipe. *Open*—
switched to *Kindle*—the hot smoke from the firebox travels
under the top of the stove and out the stovepipe. *Closed*—
switched to *Bake*—the damper blocks the stovepipe and
directs the smoke under the top of the stove, down the far side
of and below the oven compartment, and then up and out the
stovepipe from below. To use the oven or heat the reservoir,
the oven damper must be closed.

To be purchased is the *damper*. This is a metal disc (butter-
fly valve), pierced with holes, which fits snugly in the stovepipe
(they are sold in the same diameters as stovepipe). *Open*, it
allows the heat and smoke to flow uninterruptedly from the
stove and out the stovepipe. *Closed*, it retains the heat while
still allowing the smoke to escape. The handle on the outside
of the stovepipe corresponds to the position of the disc: ver-
tically it's open, horizontally it's closed.

> "If you've got a good draft, you can put two dampers in the
> stovepipe. This will help hold the heat better."
>   Neal Harrington, Warren, VT

Many stoves are equipped with a *water reservoir*. This is a
large tank, lined with copper, galvanized tin, or enamel
(reservoirs also were known as "coppers"), which, before there
were such things as gas or electric hot water heaters, provided an ever-ready supply of hot water for cooking and
washing. Other stoves may have either a *water front* or *coils;*
both make it possible to heat the domestic hot water supply.
They should be properly installed with an approved storage
tank which has a release valve, and *never* casually hooked up
to the tap water. If they are incorrectly installed, one runs the
risk of the tank or heating element exploding. To see that the
job is done right, consult a competent plumbing contractor.

Soot that has collected in the air chamber surrounding the
oven is removed through the *oven clean-out*. Usually this is
located either beneath the *oven door*, or under a removable
metal plate at the base of the oven compartment.

Warming ovens are the closed compartments above the cooking surface. Some stoves have them, others don't. They retain

some of the rising heat and are useful for storing food or things when a gentle heat is needed. *Warming shelves* are also located above the stove top: there is usually one that is nearly equal to the length of the stove; and there may be two smaller *trivets*, one at each end, that pivot to sit over the cooking surface.

Cookstove Tools

For smooth operating, the following tools will be necessary:

A lid lifter is designed to fit in a lid's notch so that the lid can be harmlessly and easily lifted. On many, the handle is loosely enclosed by a spiral of metal to protect you from the hot bar.

A soot scraper is a rectangular blade, about one by three inches, which is attached to a long metal rod. Usually the end is hooked for hanging. This is used to root around in the air passage surrounding the oven and pull out the soot and ashes. (If you don't find one to buy, they're easy to make. Weld the rectangular piece onto a ¼-inch metal rod and bend the handle.)

A fire poker is used to remove ashes from the grate, to push around sticks of wood or to spread the coals.

A grate bolt crank is used, on those stoves so designed, to tip the grates and spill the ashes.

A coal or ash shovel is needed to feed the coal and remove the ashes. (Any small shovel will do.)

An ash bucket is necessary for receiving ashes. (Any metal bucket will do.)

Potholders are necessary for the obvious reasons.

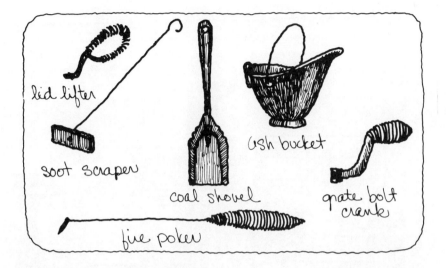

lid lifter

soot scraper

ash bucket

coal shovel

grate bolt crank

fire poker

A fire extinguisher is a must. Any ABC dry chemical or Purple K extinguisher will put out a wood fire. Also ask your fire department if they sell "chimney flares," a special flare designed to extinguish chimney fires. Not recommended are Soda and Acid or Co_2 extinguishers. Though they may calm the flames, because the first contains water and the second is a coolant, there is a good chance they'll crack the flue tiles.

GETTING THE STOVE

If you don't already own a wood cookstove, and want to do so, the second decision is whether to buy a new or old one. It's helpful to be aware of what basic qualities belong to each as you decide what kind you want to have.

New Stoves

If you buy a new stove, it's going to work. Unlike many used stoves, it isn't sold with any rust, leaks, or missing parts. New stoves come in a variety of models, from gracefully contoured traditional to cabinet-like modern, and some manufacturers even offer a range of colors from which to choose. The only criticisms I have heard include their cost—most are expensive—and the occasional long waits before receiving an order. Also, some people claim that the American-alloyed cast iron is not as durable as that used in older stoves; that the new American stoves now warp more easily and the joints are more likely to spread. But for every complaint, there's a satisfied customer.

Below is a list of both American and European stove manufacturers: if any should be of interest, the company will be able to refer you to the nearest dealer.

* Companies with an asterisk* are *out of business*, but you may still find their stoves at auctions, flea markets, or private sales.

AMERICAN

The Atlanta Stove Works
P.O. Box 5254
Atlanta, GA 30307

Model 15-36: Stove black finish with four 8-inch cooking lids and two 5-inch lids; with or without warming ovens; burns wood and coal.

11

Model 8316: Four 8-inch cooking lids; stove black finish; burns wood only.

Autocrat Corporation
New Athens, IL 62264

Hillcrest Range: Full enamel finish; six 8-inch cooking lids or two lids and two griddles; water reservoir; burns wood or coal.

Ridgetop Range: Semi-enamel finish; six 8-inch cooking lids; with or without warming shelf; burns wood or coal.

Noble Steel Cooks: Small, especially built for use by ranchers, sheepmen and overland travelers. Steel body, four 7-inch cooking lids; burns wood or coal.

Kitchen Heater: White enamel finish; one 8-inch cooking lid and one 10⅞ x 8⅞-inch griddle; burns soft coal, wood, cobs or trash.

Martin Industries
Sheffield, AL 35660

The Perfection Cook Stove Model 8-16: Stove black finish: four cooking lids; burns wood only.

Also a variety of wood burning space heaters with large cast-iron tops which provide space for cooking.

Monarch Kitchen Appliances *
Malleable Iron Range Company
Beaver Dam, WI 53916

Model R9GW: White enamel finish; two 8-inch cooking lids and two griddles; water reservoir; burns wood or coal.

Model HG36HW: White enamel finish; combination wood/coal and gas; two 8¼-inch wood/coal cooking lids and four gas burners; gas oven.

Model CE119Y-1: White enamel finish: combination coal/wood and electric; two coal/wood cooking lids and four electric units; "duo-oven"—bakes with coal/wood or electricity or in combination: an electric control set to desired oven temperature will cause electric heat to take over if wood or coal fire dies down.

Model 24PY-1: White enamel kitchen heater with two cooking lids; burns wood or coal.

Portland Stove Foundry Company
P.O. Box 1156
Portland, ME 04104

Atlantic Wood Cook Stove: Stove black finish; four 8-inch cooking lids; burns wood only.

Queen Atlantic: Several models which vary from stove black finish to a choice of different colored enamel finishes; warming shelves or warming ovens; with or without water reservoir; with or without hot water front; six 8-inch cooking lids; burns wood or coal.

CANADIAN
Elmira Stove Works
22 Church Street West
Elmira, Ontario, Canada N3B 1M3

Elmira Oval Cookstove (page 4): Comes with and without reservoir (50 in./39 in.), nickel trim. Black, almond, or gold porcelain panels; porcelain oven; top warming cabinet. Six 9¼ in. lids, one multi-lid. Solid copper water reservoir, 8 gallons with side tap. Firebox: 9" wide × 15" deep × 22" long. Depth adjustable to 8 in. for summer. Height: 62 in.; width: 29½ in. Optional water jacket heats 10 gallons running water per hour. Burns coal or wood.

EUROPEAN
Lange Ranges
American Distributor: Scandinavian Stoves *
Box 72
Alstead, NH 03602

Black cast-iron or red, blue, or green enamel finish; old-fashioned looks; large firebox; four lids; large front-loading door. Burns wood or coal.

Styria Ranges
American Distributor: The Merry Music Box*
20 McKown Street
Boothbay Harbor, ME

Three different models, all similar except one has a towel rack on three sides. All have an enamel finish, a large steel cooking surface with one removable lid, a hot water reservoir, and a fuel drawer. Burns wood, coal, charcoal, and burnable trash.

Tiba Stoves·
American Distributor: Scandinavian Stoves, Inc.*
Box 72
Alstead, NH 03602

Available in a wide variety of enameled colors; large, cast-iron cooking surface which is finned underneath for maximum heat exchange; provides domestic hot water supply; burns wood or coal.

Tirolia Solid Fuel Ranges
American Distributor: "Old Country" Appliances*
　　　　　　　　　　　P.O. Box 330
　　　　　　　　　　　Vacaville, CA 95688

Four different models and sizes; enamel finish; burn wood, coal or burnable trash.

Old Stoves

If you hold sacred the notion of owning and operating an old cookstove, you're in for many delights—and possibly a few frustrations.

Although many of the new stoves duplicate some traditional models, they don't embrace the variety and imagination displayed in the designs of older stoves. Nor can they duplicate the history. In buying an old stove, you can look for an assortment of features: plain or highly decorated front, side and back panels; warming shelves, warming ovens or ornate trivets; two to eight cooking lids, some with removable concentric rings; a thermometer on the oven door; a hot water front or reservoir; coal and/or wood grates; stove black or enamel finish; solid or isinglass panels on the oven door; with or without storage drawers underneath the oven. Some stoves even had two ovens!

The energy crunch has revived interest in the cookstove and in so doing, has elevated what used to be considered just an old piece of junk to "antique" status. Hence what a few years ago was hauled to the dump is now often selling for hundreds of dollars.

WHERE TO LOOK

Since so many of the old stoves have found new purposes in kitchens as far-ranging as backwoods-homestead to urban-quaint-chic, you may have difficulty finding the style you want for sale. The most promising and reliable place to look is a store that specializes in stoves. Its prices are more likely to be fair, and it is a place to turn to if anything goes wrong. Auctions, junk and antique stores are other sources; should they bring no luck, try advertising in the newspaper. If you live in the country or in a small town, often the local radio station has a "swap and buy" program, an excellent place to advertise.

Ask neighbors and shopkeepers if they know of anyone who might be willing to sell one. With enough patience and poking around, you may happen upon an old-timer who owns an old stove which is no longer in use: if you take your time and conceal your eagerness, you just may get what you want.

WHEN YOU FIND ONE

In the initial joy of locating a fine-looking old stove, don't lay down your money without first giving the stove a thorough examination. I know of one man who, at an auction several years ago, cheerfully paid $50 for a lavishly-scrolled, highly-polished black cookstove. It was carefully loaded into the back of his pickup, but when he got home, it lay scattered in half a dozen pieces. The owner had cunningly puttied together the broken parts and applied a stout coat of stove blacking. Be willing to spend fifteen minutes or more going over the entire stove, inspecting for the presence and soundness of all the parts. (Be sure to take a flashlight along on stove-hunting expeditions: a careful examination of the inside is as important as the outside.)

A desirable stove is one that is tight enough to prevent air from entering through any place other than the drafts; otherwise the rate of burning can't be controlled and the firebox may overheat. Also, there should be no place for the smoke to escape other than through the stovepipe.

Most old stoves are less than perfect, but some are easily repaired. Others require more work, and still others are best forgotten. Missing parts are becoming increasingly difficult to replace, and should a stove be without such functional pieces as cooking lids, T's, dividers, doors and dampers, consider moving on—or try writing to the following company which still carries some old stove parts.

Empire Furnace & Stove Repair Co.
793-797 Broadway
Albany, New York 12207

When requesting a part from this company, give them the following information: complete name of stove; correct model number; name of manufacturer; approximate age of stove; a careful description of the part needed; a rough sketch with dimensions; the old part (if you have it) which you wish replaced; a description of the casting marks on the needed part as well as on any other parts. This company is swamped with orders, so be patient.

WHAT TO LOOK FOR AND
LOOK OUT FOR

1. Check the top of the stove. Make sure all the pieces are there, that they're not warped. Look for any cracks.

Stove top cracks, if small, can be welded or brazed. Larger cracks should be reinforced underneath with a steel plate. If the T's are badly warped, (the parts most likely to do so), they'll have to be replaced, or you can try this simple repair. Fill the groove of the T, where the lid fits on, with *furnace cement* (found in hardware stores). While the cement is still wet, set the T in place, completely coat the cement with wood ashes, and put back the cooking lids. The cement will dry conforming to the shape of the lids and create an airtight seal which the warping destroys. The ashes prevent the cement from adhering to the lids.

2. Check the sides, back, bottom and base of the stove. There should be no cracks or rusted-out areas.

   Small cracks can be welded or brazed and, if necessary, re-inforced with a steel plate. If larger sections are missing, especially in such tricky areas as a curve, the problem increases. A piece of brick or screen can be fitted from behind to fill the space and then stove cement applied to fill out the front. If any parts are not securely fastened, bolts are rusted out or the seams are loose, they must be removed, cleaned and reassembled. Scrape out the old cement from the seams, re-cement with new, replace the parts and tighten with new bolts.

3. Remove the lids over the firebox and check the grates and firebox liner, making sure that they're there; that they're not warped or cracked; and that, if you plan to burn coal, the grate is the shaker type.

   A warped, cracked, or missing grate and liner can be replaced. *To replace a grate:* take a piece of cardboard and cut it to fit *loosely* on the ledge where the grate normally sits. A machine shop can cut a piece of ½-inch plate steel to match its dimensions. Then burn or drill holes, about the size of a quarter, every few inches on the side over the fire. This will make a durable, poker-type grate.

   To replace a liner: cut a piece of cardboard to fit inside the firebox along the oven wall. A piece of ¼-inch plate steel can be patterned after this and, if necessary, (some stoves require that the liner be bolted into place, but mine sits loose) bolted with *one* bolt. A patch expands differently from the stove, and if more than one bolt is used, the stress could become so great that the cast iron could crack.

To burn wood on a coal grate: Place a heavy wire screen over the coal grate, or, for a more permanent conversion, have a wood grate made (as described above) to sit on top, or replace the coal grate. These measures are only necessary if the wood coals drop through the grate too easily, or the fire is hard to control.

4. Remove the remaining lids and check the firebox wall and top of the oven for cracks.

   A firebox crack, either on the outside or oven side, deserves careful attention. If not severe, it can be filled with stove cement, then lined with a piece of sheet asbestos, and finally backed with steel plate. Again, use only one bolt to tighten it.

   Sometimes the metal has been so badly burnt that it has deteriorated to the point of uselessness. If the stove looks suspicious and you cannot determine this yourself, have somebody who knows metal look over the stove before you buy it.

5. Open the oven door and check the walls and top for any cracks or rusted-out areas.

   These can be welded or brazed, or covered with ¼-inch plate steel, and tightened into place with as few bolts as possible.

6. Check all the seams of the stove to insure that they're tight-fitting.

   A gaping seam, besides being difficult to repair, in-dicates there is something wrong with the stove or that it has, sometime in the past, been heartlessly dropped or abused.

7. All the moving parts—doors, dampers, draft slides and

levers—should be in place, closely fitting, and easily moved.

Missing doors, especially flat-fitting ones, can sometimes be replaced with a door fashioned out of steel. Doors with rounded contours are more difficult to fit.

Household oil, penetrating oil, and kerosene will usually loosen stiff joints.

8. If the stove has a water reservoir, check the cast iron supporting it to make sure that it's sound. Some of the stove companies didn't make vents for the steam to escape; instead the moisture collected on the inside of the reservoir cover, condensed, and rolled around the reservoir tank into the hot air chamber below. This water would combine with ashes, which had blown over from the firebox, to produce lye. After years of use, the lye would corrode the end of the stove. This must be repaired before the stove can be used.

   Also check to see that the reservoir liner is there; a missing or damaged one can be replaced with a liner made of galvanized tin or copper.

9. Check for rust damage. There likely will be some rust, but if it's only on the surface, it's harmless and easy to remove. Some stoves, however, were stored without first being cleaned of ashes, and the moisture accumulation and ashes will have eaten thin parts of the metal. So, if the inside of the stove looks like a lace curtain, forget it.

   For heavily surface-rusted stoves, sandblasting is an effective and time-saving solution. Often, gravestone and monument makers provide this service. One stove repairer I know, however, insists on removing the layers by

---

"I don't like to use kerosene on a stove because it streaks cast iron. Parts that have soaked up the kerosene won't polish up the same as the rest of the stove after it's blacked."

Allen Hill, Johnson, VT

hand (with a wire brush attachment on a power drill) as it encourages a careful examination of the stove. Thin layers of rust are removed with steel wool.

10. For those parts that need replating, look in the Yellow Pages under "Plating." Most old stoves were plated with the dull, yellowish nickel (there is a choice of dull or shiny). Chrome is also an alternative: it is bluer in color and doesn't require as much polishing. Whatever you choose, however, don't first sandblast or grind the part. Simply take it as is, rust and all.

11. Look for makeshift repairs. They will appear as gray or rough areas. Furnace cement which has been used to fill in cracks or fill out missing pieces of metal will not take stove blacking the same as metal.

These recommendations for stove repairs may or may not be helpful for your particular problems; I have discovered that for every person versed in stove repairs, there is a somewhat different solution. But unless you're an experienced welder or repair person, you would be smart to seek out someone who is. There are countless stories of jury-rigged repairs which led to fires far grander than what the firebox held. Anything which involves a fire inside your home requires utmost care.

TRANSPORTING THE STOVE

Many old stoves are in bad shape because of the way they were handled. Cast iron is often described as being "as fragile as glass," so it must be treated accordingly. Before moving a stove, take off all the removable parts—lids, T's, dividers, doors, etc.—wrap them in paper and pack them in cardboard boxes. Lift the stove from its sturdiest points—and not, let's say, from the water reservoir. Set the stove on a mat, boards, or tires, resting it on its back. Never transport it upright or a leg may break en route. Secure the stove with rope so that it doesn't bang around, and once you're there, at all costs, avoid dropping it.

ONCE IT'S IN PLACE

The acid test for determining the soundness of your stove—once it's connected to the chimney—is to build a slow and easy fire in the firebox. Stay there and listen to the snaps and cracks. Cast iron, as it expands with the heat, makes pleasant little ticking sounds; but if you should hear something that cracks with more authority, look for the problem. Parts that are under tension will, as they expand, make themselves known. Leaks will be revealed by unwanted smoke escaping into the room. (To start a fire, refer to the chapter on "Getting the Fire Going"—this chapter also outlines other reasons for a smoking stove.)

BLACKING

The final step in revitalizing an unenameled cast-iron stove (and the cooking surface of an enameled stove) is to black it. Not only does blacking enhance the appearance, but also it retards rust and helps a stove to throw out heat better.

There are two basic types of blacking, paste and liquid. *Paste* blacking is rubbed on with a soft cloth; it is said to be more durable than the liquid, but its application—especially if there's much detailed decoration—takes more time. The *liquid* blacking must be stirred with a stick (the part that "blacks" settles to the bottom of the container), poured into a can, and brushed on much like paint. If the stove is slightly warm, the liquid blacking will dry more quickly after its application. Both types can be polished with a nylon bristle brush, a shoe brush, or with a wire brush attachment on a power drill. With whichever blacking, you must, according to a friend, "Scrub the hell out of it." Also advisable is to put down newspapers or a drop cloth for the blacking and the polishing. Liquid blacking easily splashes, and polishing produces copious amounts of graphite dust. It's quite predictable that both the work area and the worker will get pretty dirty.

Don't be alarmed if your stove smokes and smells of tar after it has been blacked. Usually one firing is needed to burn off the residue, but these unpleasant aftereffects are short-lasting.

SETTING UP

Before you set the stove in place, first determine where it should sit, what safety precautions are necessary, and check to make sure the chimney is safe. Your back will be straighter and your house more secure.

Location

For peak efficiency and minimal maintenance, the stove should be placed so that the shortest and most direct span of stovepipe is used to connect it to the chimney. This creates the most expedient path for establishing a good draft and heating the *chimney flue* (the shaft through which the smoke passes)—a condition necessary for reducing the accumulation of creosote and soot.

Yet for optimal radiation of heat, the stove should occupy the center of the room. Not only is there more air circulating around the stove but also the extra lengths of stovepipe needed to connect it to the chimney will give off added heat. This is a trade-off, though: longer horizontal spans of stovepipe accelerate creosote build-up, and more frequent stovepipe cleanings will be necessary. And there are limits to the length of this horizontal span; it will depend on strength of the chimney draft, the wood that is burned, and the stove itself. There are no rules; you'll just have to experiment with your own set-up to see what works best.

If the stove is equipped with either a hot water front or coils which are to be hooked up to one or more storage tanks, consideration must be given to their location.

23

According to guidelines prepared by the National Fire Protection Association, a cookstove should be placed so that the back and firebox side maintain a distance of three feet from any unprotected combustible wall or surface; the oven side must be at least eighteen inches away. If suitable protective wall coverings are used, however, these distances can be significantly reduced. Sheet metal, ¼-inch asbestos millboard,* metal-lined asbestos stove boards, and decorative, non-flammable wall panels (all available at hardware stores) permit a closer proximity to the wall as long as they're installed with at least one to two inches of air space between them and the wall—or according to manufacturer's instructions—and supported by non-flammable spacers. Though fire resistant, most of these materials do conduct heat and without adequate air space behind, there is the possibility of charring or igniting the wall.

The NFPA also recommends safe clearances for mounting stoves on the floor. If there is at least eighteen inches of open space between the stove and floor, no protective floor covering is necessary; for anything less, it is. Suitable floor mounts range from building a raised hearth of bricks, tiles, fieldstones, or concrete blocks to simply laying down asbestos millboard or metal-lined asbestos stove board.

In many old New England farmhouses, the cooking and eating were done in the same room. This was well-intended in the winter, when the stove's heat was needed, but by summer it became uncomfortable. Rather than moving to another room to eat, however, the cooking was done in another place—the summer kitchen. This room, often located "out back," provided the additional space for preserving the harvests of garden and barnyard, the making of butter and cheese, and the fall ritual of boiling down cider—an affair almost as steamy as making maple syrup.

Cost and space make summer kitchens impractical today, but I know several cooks who annually move their stoves

---

*Do not mistake asbestos millboard for asbestos cement board or transite, as they are hazardous and should not be used.

outside (some have an extra stove just for this purpose), protect them with construction-tarp ceilings, and escape the heat
of the house for the coolness of the outdoors. Apart from keeping out moisture, the only other problem is keeping out
animals. I spent one summer cooking in an outdoor kitchen,
one which included not only the stove but also a sink and
cupboard full of food. It took the raccoons no time at all to
figure out how to open the cupboard doors, and they cele-
brated their first B & E by devouring the two packages of wild
rice I had been hoarding for some dazzling occasion. There
was a cheerful ending to this outrage, however; one of the
thieves became so enamored of our menu that he would appear
each night for a share of the meal, which he learned to
accept politely from our hands.

Stovepipe Installation

Stovepipe safety begins with the selection of stovepipe.
Black pipe, or blued steel, is intended for interiors, galvanized
sheet metal pipe for outdoors. (Though the galvanized is
sturdier and longer-lasting, it can give off harmful gases under
extreme heat.) If you buy or find used pipes, check them for
any rust or corrosion; thin areas are always a threat but become
particularly hazardous in the event of a chimney fire, when
they could wear through completely.

Below is a list of basic rules for connecting a stove to a
chimney: if you have further questions, there are various
books, as well as bulletins issued by the National Fire Protection Association (470 Atlantic Ave., Boston, MA 02210)
which are excellent guides. And most fire departments have a
list of safety codes which they gladly will share.

* Use a stovepipe that is the same diameter as the stove
  collar. If the chimney opening is too small, enlarge it
  rather than reducing the size of the pipe as that also would
  reduce the draft.

* Draft is mainly dependent on chimney height and the diameter of the flue: the higher the chimney and larger the diameter, the greater the draft. To help insure proper draft:

  a. Make sure the diameter of the flue is 25 percent greater than the stovepipe.

  b. Use the shortest and most direct span of stovepipe to connect the stove to the chimney: the more elbow pieces in the connection, the worse the draft. However, if you plan a long span of stovepipe, there should be at least ¼-inch of upward slant to the chimney per running foot of pipe. At no point should the stovepipe be higher than the chimney opening which it should enter horizontally, extending only to the inner face of the flue, and not so far as to block the draft. To test for good draft, stick a ball of crushed newspapers—the size of the stovepipe—into the chimney opening and set it on fire. If the paper is drawn up the chimney, the draft is good. If it is not, inspect the chimney for loose bricks, mortar, or air leaks.

* If possible, connect only one stove or heating device per chimney, and never, according to the NFPA, connect a stove to a flue serving a fireplace unless the hearth is sealed shut. This is to prevent flue gases and sparks from entering a room. Also, two or more heating devices may reduce the amount of draft, cause the stoves to smoke, and lead to a quicker accumulation of creosote. However, if a common chimney is unavoidable, space the flue openings at different elevations, block off any unused openings,

"If you don't know what you're doing, don't start. A stove is only as safe as the way it's hooked up."

Allen Hill, Johnson, VT

and make certain that the flue is of a large enough diameter to provide adequate draft.

* Insert a stovepipe damper in the first section of pipe—or in the first section which can be reached handily.

* Fit a metal thimble (a flat ring sold in the same diameters as stovepipes) snugly around the stovepipe where it enters the chimney so that it lies flat against the opening. This will prevent a back puff from dislodging the pipe from the chimney. Stove cement applied around the joint accomplishes the same thing but prevents removing the stovepipe for easy cleaning.

* Fit together the sections of stovepipe so that the crimped ends slide into the smooth ends, and face *towards* the stove; in the event of drooling creosote, the gooey mess will run into the stove rather than onto the floor. (I learned this the hard way and have stained woodwork to prove it.)

* For greater security, stovepipe sections—especially long ones—should be fastened together with short sheet metal screws. Using a nail as a center punch, mark three holes for each joint, drill, and insert screws.

* There should be a clearance of at least eighteen inches between the stovepipe and any flammable surface (this includes wall, ceilings, cabinets, furniture, etc.). To set the stovepipe any closer, a protective liner must be fastened to the surface—again, leave a one- to two-inch air space between the wall and liner. Check with your fire department or insurance company to determine just how close the stovepipe can be to the liner.

* If the stovepipe penetrates a wall or other flammable surface, the diameter of the opening should be cut eighteen inches wider than the diameter of the stovepipe, and lined with firebrick, asbestos, insulated UL listed all-fuel chimney pipe, or other non-combustible material. Remember, keep flammable materials, such as wallpaper, away from the stovepipe.

Chimneys

Smoky chimneys had been a problem since their very beginning, which has been traced to several English castles built in the twelfth century. In early New England, there flourished a trade known as chimney doctoring: certain self-acknowledged professionals claimed to cure the ills of a smoky chimney; by all accounts they succeeded only in duping their clients for a fee and the smoke continued to bring tears to the eyes. But you should have none of these problems. As long as there is enough draft, the flue is unobstructed, the construction is tight, the chimney is of a proper height and width, and the stove is properly connected, the chimney will effortlessly perform the job for which it was designed.

If you intend to use an existing chimney, it must be checked for soundness. Inspect masonry chimneys—inside and out—for cracks (which appear as dark lines in the soot), loose mortar and bricks. A chimney that isn't tight produces a poor draft and could cause a fire to spread into the house. One method for testing the solidity of the construction is to try to insert the blade of a knife into the mortar and into one of the bricks itself. (The basement, where the bricks are damp, is a good place to conduct this experiment.) If the blade penetrates the materials, they are weak and the chimney is unsafe.

Another test for determining the tightness of the chimney is first to drive out the cold air in the flue by burning a few sheets of newspaper, then throw a packet of wet newspapers over the

"Although chimneys have been building for a 1,000 years, the artisans of the present day seem strangely ignorant of the true method of constructing them so as always to carry smoke upward instead of downward. The writer in early life shed many a bitter tear, drawn forth by smoke from an ill-constructed kitchen-chimney, and thousands all over the land can report the same experience."

Miss Beecher's Housekeeper and Healthkeeper, 1874

top of the flue, and finally start a smudge fire in the stove. Look and sniff for escaping smoke.

Before burning a fire in the stove, the chimney flue must be checked for soot, creosote, and other obstructions. Not only is it likely that there will be some chimney deposits to remove, but it's possible that an inactive chimney may have attracted home-hunting birds or squirrels. Our local fire chief recalled one incident when either grackles or chimney swifts had nested in an idle chimney over the summer and when the unsuspecting owner lit the season's first fire, he also ignited the masses of abandoned bedding and straw. What was intended just to take off the chill nearly succeeded in leveling his house.

To check for nests, creosote buildup, and any bricks that may have come loose, insert a hand mirror into the chimney clean out opening. If you cannot see daylight reflected in the mirror, you've got trouble (or a cap installed on the chimney top). If creosote and soot are your problems, refer to the chapter on "Care and Cleaning" for chimney cleaning methods; if fallen bricks are the problem, seek the help of a good mason.

New chimneys can be constructed from stone, brick, concrete block, or pre-fabricated metal chimney kits—the choice is dependent on taste, time, and the amount of money one is willing to spend. Some of the first chimneys in the New England colonies were made of wood; logs or sticks were piled together at right angles, and the cracks filled with clay and mortar. These chimneys were not long-lasting, nor, do I imagine, were the houses on which they were constructed, as the roofs were thatched with reeds.

For greater heat retention, chimneys should be located inside the house rather than along an outside wall. A masonry chimney absorbs heat and will continue to radiate warmth into the room long after the fire has gone out. An interior chimney also improves the performance of the stove: each time the fire is lit, there is not the freezing column of air to force out before a good draft can be established, and by having a warmer flue lining, there is less condensation of wood moisture and vapors which cause the build-up of creosote. If conditions prevent the building of an interior chimney, try to choose a southern location for an exterior chimney; the exposure to the sun and protection from the chilling north winds will increase its efficiency.

A masonry chimney should be constructed so that it is supported on a concrete or masonry foundation, or such that the ground bears its weight rather than the building. And see that it is sunk below frost level, or the construction may heave. The flue should have a diameter of at least nine inches (the cross-section of the flue should be 25 percent greater than the stovepipe to be used), and be built with fire clay flue tiles or with other material that can resist corrosion, softening, or cracking from flue gases that reach temperatures up to 1800° F. And the tiles should be laid so that they're tight fitting and the flue surface is even and smooth. Either hire a good mason, or, if you're building the chimney yourself, carefully consult chimney building guides.

Factory-built metal chimneys should be put up according to manufacturer's instructions. They go up more quickly and easily than masonry chimneys and provide a handy solution to the problem of needing a chimney in a hurry. One January we acquired a heating stove but had no chimney through which to vent it; three days later, with the help of a friend and a pre-fab chimney, we were sitting in the living room warming ourselves by the fire. Another advantage of a metal chimney is that the flue heats up quickly, keeping creosote to a minimum.

To insure adequate draft and a safe roof, the chimney top should terminate at least three feet above where it passes through the roof of a building and at least two feet higher than any portion of a building within ten feet. Downdrafts often occur if the house is surrounded by tall trees or if it sits in a depression in the land; the wind blows over the trees or hills and down into the chimney, forcing the smoke back into the room. To correct this, the chimney may have to be extended or, more simply, it may have only to be fitted with a chimney cap, which perches atop the chimney looking very much like a Chinese coolie's hat. This also keeps out rain and snow and is a worthwhile investment for any chimney.

If you're installing a chimney yourself, be sure to allow for proper clearances when going through floors and ceilings.

There have been scores of homeless stove owners who had proceeded without precaution and care.

And as a final warning, don't set flammable materials—tinder, matches, rugs, magazines, furniture—near the stove. The most cautiously installed stove could cause the most damage if flammable objects are left within firing range.

Increasing Heat Radiation

Though most wood cookstoves should never have to double as heating devices (over-firing the range could cause the surface to warp and the grate to burn out), their heating performance can be improved by observing the following rules:

* Keep the oven damper closed: this causes more of the stove's surface to heat up, thus increasing the heat radiated into the room.
* Use a longer stovepipe to connect the range to the chimney. (Remember the trade-off: more heat for more creosote.)
* A large screen of crinkled aluminum foil placed behind the stove will reflect heat in all directions.
* A long, shallow metal container filled with sand and placed under the stove will absorb heat and add extra warmth to the room.
* A small fan installed behind the stove will improve the circulation of air heated by the stove.
* Leaving the oven door open will throw off more heat.

FUEL SUPPLY

Firing a kitchen range today means using one of two fuels: wood or coal. A century earlier, however, stoves were often fueled by what was immediately at hand. In the treeless prairie states, the homesteaders first relied upon dried cow or buffalo dung, so-called "prairie coal," to feed their stoves. But as more people arrived, the cows and the buffalos couldn't produce fast enough to meet the increasing need for fuel, and new energy sources were sought.

In 1871, an advertisement appeared advocating the use of sunflower seeds, claiming that "one acre of land would produce twelve cords and furnish enough fuel for the winter."* However, the most popular—and no doubt more manageable—outgrowth of this search for fuel was hay, the land's most abundant commodity. The hay was twisted into log-sized bundles, or "cats," which provided an intense though short-lived fire which was adequate for heating and cooking. But as the cultivation of corn expanded, corncobs replaced hay as the principle source of fuel. They became equally abundant and their fire was longer-lasting. It was the use of these two fuels which took credit for protecting so many prairie lives during the unexpected, devastating blizzard in 1888.

Tremendous gains were made in the next eighty years—from buffalo chips to microwaves—but those of us who want to be independent of outside energy sources, or who want to recapture the flavor of the past, are turning to wood.

---

*Josephine H. Pierce, *Fire on the Hearth,* The Pond-Ekberb Co., 1951, p. 192.

Woods for Cooking and Heating

There is a popular expression among health-food advocates which says, "You are what you eat." Similarly the theme for fueling a cookstove might be, "You are what you burn." If you understand how your stove works, if it is kept free of soot and ashes, and has a good draft, your fire will determine how the stove cooks.

Fuel woods must provide a wide range of intensity and duration of heat to accommodate different types of cooking: a hot blaze for stir-frying; a moderate to hot heat for top-of-the-range cooking; a steady, even heat for baking and roasting; a bed of glowing coals for broiling. When you are ready to cut or buy wood, match the needs of your cooking with the burning and heating properties of different woods. Generally, this is the way it is:

Kindling: Softwoods, such as *poplar, aspen, spruce, fir, pine,* and *balsam* are good. Coniferous softwoods contain greater amounts of resins than hardwoods, causing them to ignite faster and burn hotter, but for a shorter time. Kindling should be split to the size of a broom handle. Other kindling material includes dead twigs of softwood trees, pine cones, dried citrus peels, dried corn cobs, and hardwood splinters from the splitting block.

"All woods are good for something. Nature put them there for us; we just have to learn how to use them."
Perry Wilder, Colrain, MA

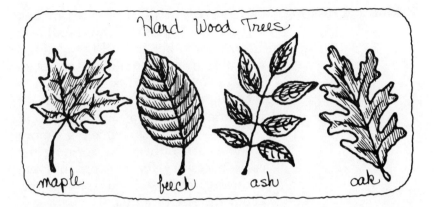

General top-of-the-range:	Hardwoods are usually best, and most any will do. They should be split to about two to three inches square.
	Ash is very good; it produces a hot, long-lasting flame and burns when still green.
	Soft maple (red maple) produces a quick flame and delivers moderate heat.
	Black and yellow birch produce a quick, hot fire; *white birch* is mediocre fuel; and *gray birch* is best forgotten.
	Beech, sugar maple, black cherry, apple, and *hophornbeam* are good, hot, all-around woods.
Stir-frying:	Finely split *white birch* produces the quick, hot flames desirable for this type of cooking, but any of the above, finely split, will work.
Broiling:	Any of the woods suggested for baking are good, except the birches. *Apple* and other fruit woods are particularly well-suited as they release a special fragrance which flavors the food. In this case, the size stick doesn't matter as much as well-formed coals.

Baking and roasting: *Hickory, oak, black locust, apple,* and *dogwood* are superior. They produce a slow, steady, hot fire: all the qualities desirable for maintaining an even heat over long cooking times when a set temperature is required. Any of the other hardwoods will do, except *white* and *gray birch,* which go more easily to ash rather than forming the coals necessary for making an even, enduring heat. Use unsplit pieces, about the size of a salami.

Long, slow cooking: Any unsplit hardwood will do, though denser woods, such as *hickory, oak, black locust, hophornbeam* and *dogwood* will burn more slowly.

If you're going to be using your cookstove for heating as well as cooking, use the table below which lists the approximate fuel values for different woods.

Species	Million Btu's per air-dry 90 cu. ft. wood
Black locust	26.5
Shagbark hickory	25.4
Hophornbeam	24.7
White oak	23.9
Sugar maple	21.8
Beech	21.8
Red oak	21.7
Yellow birch	21.3
White ash	20.0
Red maple	19.1
Black cherry	18.5
White birch	18.2
White elm	17.7
Red spruce	15.0
Hemlock	15.0
White pine	13.3

And if you want to send pleasant aromas into the air—apart from what you're cooking—here is an article from *The New York Times* which speaks of the fragrances of different woods:

> Each fire—one might say fireplace—has its own aroma. Birch, for instance, is a kindling wood of short fire but full of flavor; its bark alone can savor a whole evening. Ash is more pungent and more enduring, but its fragrance is even stronger in the woodbox than on the coals. Apple, or almost any fruit wood, is aromatic in its own right, and double so in flames.
>
> Cedar is full of sparks and explosive outbursts, and its fire dies quickly; but while it lives and threatens every rug in reach, it is fragrant as the very mountains. Oak, of course, is the sturdy backlog, pungent as leather and smelling wintry, for the oak fire is a fire for long nights when snow creaks underfoot and frost bites deep.

There are two generally recognized rules for burning fuel wood. The first is that *softwoods are for kindling, hardwoods for cooking.* The resins which so well suit coniferous softwoods for starting a fire are what discourage them from extending one. They quickly contribute to a build-up of creosote and soot and make more frequent chimney cleanings necessary. Also, softwoods contain greater numbers of air pockets which, when heated, expand and explode, sending sparks up the chimney. Should one of these sparks catch in some of the unburned material lining the chimney wall, there is the chance that it will start a fire.

The second rule says that *wood should be seasoned (dried) if it is to be an effective wood for cooking and heating.* I have heard old-time stove users claim that two-year wood burns best, but most of us can't wait so long. Do allow it at least six months of seasoning, and if possible, let it go another six. The reason for this is that heat is needed to vaporize the moisture in the burning wood before the wood can be broken down into gases, volatiles, and charcoal. The energy needed to drive off the moisture serves only that purpose and the wood's heating value for cooking food or warming a room is lost. Consequently, the greater the quantity of moisture in burning wood, the greater the heating loss. Whereas the weight of dry wood is about 20 percent water, some green wood contains up to 78 percent.

And if such a significant energy loss weren't reason enough to wait those six to twelve months, green wood is also responsible for causing a faster accumulation of creosote and soot. As the vaporized moisture escapes up the chimney, it condenses and deposits its gummy remains in the stovepipe and flue. If green wood must be burned, add it finely split to a hot fire only: the hotter the stovepipe and flue, the less chance there is for condensation to occur. Never, for instance, add green wood to a slow or smouldering fire, for combustion will be incomplete—leaving behind unburned gases and volatiles—and the cooler chimney will cause a greater amount of messy and dangerous condensation. Some cooks recommend using green wood as a means for controlling heat—as for baking and roasting—and no doubt this works; but it also adds to the creosote lining your chimney and for this reason I don't suggest it.

If you're caught having to burn unseasoned wood, use ash, yellow birch, black birch, beech, or sumac. Of most freshly cut woods, these seem to burn the best.

Dry wood can be recognized by the many cracks which radiate from the core towards the bark. And the sharp, precise cracking sound produced when two dry sticks are hit together rings very differently from the dull thud of two green ones. To conclusively determine the dryness of your wood, try this experiment: Take a stick of wood, weigh it, and then cook it in a *slow* oven for a few hours. Remove it and weigh it again. This loss in weight represents moisture content; calculate to a percentage what this water weight is of the dry wood. For

example, if a block of wood weighs 1½ pounds before cooking, and 1 pound after, it lost ½ pound of water. One-half pound equals 50 percent of the final weight. Therefore, the moisture content of the block was 50 percent. An acceptable percentage would be 20 percent or less; anything more means that the wood requires more seasoning.

Don't wait so long to use your wood that it becomes punky. Rotten wood, though indeed dry, is a very poor heating and cooking wood. Some fuel woods have longer productive lives than others and each should be used before it is spent.

Where to Get Wood*

Home-grown and harvested firewood is the most economical of fuel sources. If you lack a woodlot, there are other alternatives which still make wood ranges economically attractive. Often state and municipal parks have marked cull trees that, for a minimal sum, may be cut by the public. By removing these crooked or damaged trees, more space and nutrients are available to the healthier crop.** Check hardwood logging operations; usually tops and cull logs are left. Many wood stove cooks express a preference for small branches; though inadequate for the larger fireboxes of heating stoves, they are just right for a cookstove.

Look for wood in the town dump. A particularly rewarding time is soon after telephone and electric company crews have gone around pruning roadside branches, or after a heavy storm which has knocked down trees and large limbs. Lumberyards, furniture factories, and construction sites are also likely places to pick up scrap wood. And don't forget friends and neighbors: they may have diseased or damaged trees—or a

---

*No matter where you get your wood, it should be split, stacked, and properly seasoned. These operations are not covered in this book, but are fully explained in many others. Do consult them, or someone knowledgeable in these areas, for the safest and most effective techniques.

**To get an address, check in the phone book under U.S. Government, Agriculture, Department of Forest Service, or under the Environmental Conservation Agency.

fallen limb—that need to be cleared. Gathering firewood properly is an invitation to take part in nature's balance; the search will be as much a service to the land as it is a boon for the kitchen.

BUYING WOOD

If you don't have the time or don't own a woodlot (or if you're waiting for your own wood to season), buying wood is about your only alternative. But be forewarned. Some wood dealers may try to take advantage of a greenhorn, and when a price is quoted for a cord of wood, ask to know if it's hardwood or softwood, how long it has been seasoned, and what are its dimensions (be sure that it is cut into lengths shorter than your firebox). When stacked, a cord of wood measures four feet high, four feet wide, and eight feet long. Sometimes what is passed off as a cord is actually a *face cord*, or *run*, which measures four feet high, sixteen inches wide, and eight feet long—equal to one-third of a cord. A sure way to get what you want is to make an agreement that the wood be delivered and stacked, and then paid for.

AMOUNT OF WOOD

It's difficult to predict just how much wood you'll need; that depends on how much the stove is used and what kind of wood is burned. But a fair estimate for a stove that is used nearly every day for a year, and is fueled with well-seasoned hardwood, is about five to six cords. Have seven cords to be safe (especially if you're heating the domestic water supply).

"Wood that is straight and solid makes more in a load, and is the most profitable. A cord of small crooked sticks does not contain half the wood there is in a load of solid logs. To know the amount of a load, multiply the length by the breadth, and the product by the height, and you have the number of square feet. If it is 128 feet, it is a cord."

Miss Beecher's Domestic Receipts, 1874

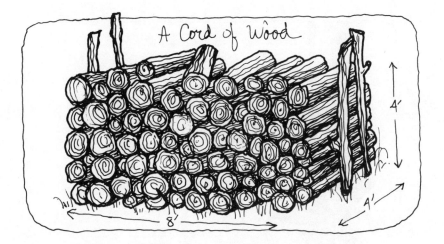

WOODBOXES

A requisite companion to any wood-burning stove is a wood-box. This you'll want to place within easy reach of the stove, but not so close that it's a fire hazard. I use an old copper boiler; it hugs the stove and holds a couple days' supply of split cooking wood. Others prefer to have larger woodboxes, which don't need filling so frequently. Whatever fits your preference and your kitchen will determine its size. I have seen one wood-box that was built without a bottom. Every so often it is emptied and lifted so that the dirt and wood chips can be swept away. Also, it is large enough to accommodate different kinds and sizes of wood: the kindling is neatly stacked on one side, general cooking wood in the middle, and a pile of hickory, used just for baking, on the far end.

Many cooks do the final splitting just before they add the sticks to the fire and so keep a small splitting block and hatchet in the kitchen. In this case, it's wise to find or design a spot to keep the hatchet out of children's reach.

> "Don't make the woodbox too big. Not only does it take up too much room, but you can never dig down for that piece of wood that's just right."
>
> Gwen Robinson, Orford, NH

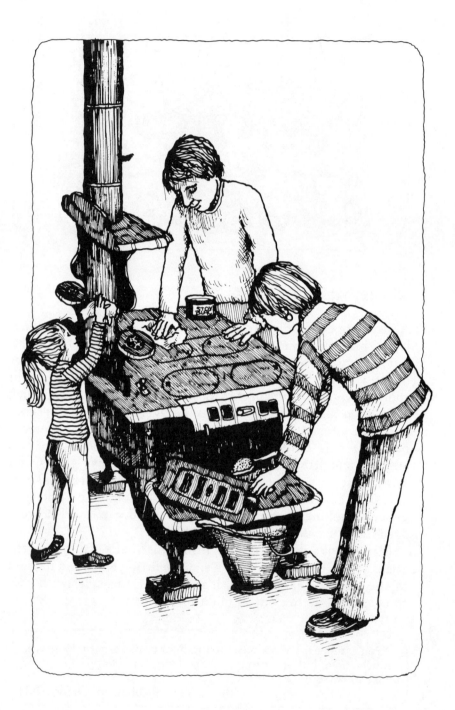

CARE AND CLEANING

The Stove

To look their best, most wood ranges (especially the black cast-iron stoves) require more attention than modern stoves; but few cooks today would put up with what was expected from housewives in 1883:

> Every morning, clean out all ashes and cinders, sift these, reserve the cinders for use and throw the dust away. Sweep away as much of the soot as can be reached with a sweep's brush kept for this purpose. Black-lead the range. (In houses where one or two servants only are kept it will, perhaps, be deemed sufficient if the bars and front of the fire only are black-leaded every day, the whole of the range being dealt with on a fixed day twice a week. Where there are several servants, the range flues should be swept out and black-leaded, and the oven scraped and washed every day.) Wash off any spilt grease with a flannel, hot water and soda, and wipe dry before black-leading. Sweep out the oven, scrape the shelves with an old knife, and wash them with vinegar and water.
>
> Clean the steelwork of the range with emery paper, or crocus powder which should be mixed with sweet oil and laid on, rubbed off when dry, and polished with leather and a little dry powder. Clean the brass-work with polishing-paste and a leather, or if badly tarnished, with oxalic acid. Wash over the hearth with a house-flannel and clear water. Then wring out the cloth, dip in whiting moistened with a little milk and pass evenly over the whole surface. Clean the fender and fire-irons with emery paper, or a flannel dipped in warm-ash-dust.
>
> Once a week, wash out the boiler, and scrape off any fur.

As a more realistic daily routine, wipe or scrape off surface spills. Grease spatters can be rubbed into the metal with either newspapers or brown paper bags; or to prevent large

43

spatters from burning while the stove is still hot, immediately cover them with ashes. After the stove has cooled, brush away ashes and the spot should be gone.

Once a week or more, when the stove is hot but not scorching, many people rub the cooking surface with wax paper (remember the paper bread bags?), petroleum jelly, or vegetable oil or lard: all will keep it rust-free, black, and shiny.

"Clean the stove top by rubbing briskly with an old clean woolen sock dipped in cold coffee. Some people used oil (kerosene) instead of coffee, but mother forbade it because of fire danger."

Shirley Sweedman, Max, MN

Black stoves will, in time, need re-blacking. Enameled stoves are cleaned much like a refrigerator. When the stove is cool, go over soiled areas with a damp sponge and a household detergent. Try to remove spills before they cook onto the surface.

Although the air chamber surrounding a wood stove oven requires more frequent cleaning than either an electric or gas oven, it can boast of collecting a different kind of dirt; rather than amassing the greasy film of the modern appliances, it accumulates a powdery, dry soot. And the oven compartment itself requires very infrequent cleaning; the spilled food probably dries out or burns up. At most, it occasionally will need sweeping out.

Before cleaning the air chamber, place newspaper on the floor as the soot is easily stirred and very messy. Insert the soot scraper into the clean-out hole and bring the soot forward from all the corners and crannies. A flashlight is helpful to check your progress. As a finishing touch, I stick in the nozzle of my vacuum cleaner and let it sniff around.

Amongst wood stove cooks there is some difference of opinion as to how thorough one should be in cleaning the oven chamber. Some claim that the top of the oven should be cleaned as thoroughly as the bottom to insure an even baking

heat; others insist that a little bit of soot helps even out the heat. I don't know if that disparity is a function of the difference in stoves or the sensitivity of the cook. I do know, though, that if the tops of your baked goods refuse to brown by the time the food is cooked, the oven top needs cleaning. Just remove the lids and dividers above and either scrape or vacuum out the soot. You'll have to work and watch your own stove to determine just how much soot to remove.

Reservoirs should be drained every so often, while the fire is either out or very low, and wiped of any lime, rust, and mineral deposits. If this task gets to be bothersome, there is a handy little trick which avoids emptying the tank. Take a clean piece of old towel or sheet and tie a small rock or weight in one corner. Drop this into the reservoir. The cloth will sink

"Mica in stoves when smoked is readily cleaned by taking it out and thoroughly washing with vinegar a little diluted. If the black does not come off at once, let it soak a while."
The Home Queen World's Fair Souvenir Cookbook, **1893**

"To purify the atmosphere of a room: Mix, in a cup, some brown sugar, with sufficient water to make a thick liquid. Put a hot coal on a shovel; pour on the coal a teaspoonful or more of the sugar and carry it carefully around the room. The smoke will entirely remove any disagreeable odour."

Miss Leslie's New Receipts for Cooking, 1874

and stay on the bottom where it will collect the deposits which leach out of the water. When the cloth becomes saturated with deposits, toss it out and replace with another.

KEEPING DOWN CREOSOTE

An efficient stove and a safe house are both dependent on controlling the amount of creosote and soot coating the stove-pipe and chimney. The greater the accumulation, the more the damper will have to be opened to prevent smoking and the greater the likelihood of a chimney fire. According to Allen Hill, of Johnson, VT, "The best way to prevent a chimney fire is to open the dampers once a day, every day, and let the fire go for about ten minutes." What this does is to create a very hot fire which reaches high into the chimney, burning up the soot deposits and blowing them out. This method is not recommended, however, if you've let weeks of soot and creosote build up, for indeed, they will burn up, but in the form of a first-rate chimney fire.

Other means for minimizing creosote include adding two to three cups of rock salt, every week or so, to a well-burning fire—potato peelings perform the same function. One long-time stove user claims that his folks always saved their potato peels for the firebox and they had fewer chimney fires than anybody else on their hill. I don't peel my potatoes, so I can't verify the claim, but for those of you who do, try chucking them in the stove rather than in the compost.

There is at least one commercial product—*Chimney Sweep*—that is designed for keeping chimneys clean. Like salt, it is applied to a vigorous fire, and also like salt, it will not remove the creosote and soot that have already accumulated; it only will help retard their build-up.

Once the creosote, tars, and soot are there, you have little option, but to clean the stovepipe and chimney. A small amount can be tolerated—it even helps seal the stovepipe—but thick, crusty coatings are a hazard and should be removed.

STOVEPIPE CLEANING

A good rapping on the pipes will loosen and knock off some of the build-up (and also indicate, by the dullness of the thud, just how much is there), but it will not really clean it. The best way I've found is to spread newspapers on the floor underneath the pipes, and pull the stovepipe out of the flue and off the stove. Carry it outside, set it in a cleared area—such as on a dirt road or in the snow—stuff it with loosely wadded newspapers and set them on fire. The burning paper will ignite the creosote and dry it up. After the fire dies, scrape the pipe's insides with a flat piece of wood or soot scraper and the pipe is ready for reinstallation.

> "If you can't close the stovepipe damper very far without it smoking, it's time to clean the stovepipe."
>
> Perry Wilder, Colrain, MA

Chimney Cleaning

The best time for cleaning chimneys is in the fall; by then the creosote has dried and become more brittle. But if you burn much green or softwood, chimney inspections should be more frequent; a clogged chimney is like playing with fire.

The simplest way to clean a chimney is to hire a chimney sweep or call the fire department (it may provide that service). But with a little more effort, you can do it yourself. One of the least complicated ways is to drop a logging chain into the chimney and wiggle and scrape it all around the sides. You also can bunch up a chain, tie a rope around it, and drop the bundle to scrape the chimney sides. Another method is to tie a weighted bag of straw to a long rope and run it up and down the shaft. Others attach two long ropes to either end of a spruce bough or small evergreen. One of the ropes is dropped into the chimney and is caught by a helper through the clean-out opening. The tree is then pulled back and forth, producing the same sort of action as a bottle brush.

If a chimney attached to a fireplace is being cleaned, first be sure to seal off the hearth to prevent clouds of black soot from descending into the room.

CHIMNEY FIRES

Despite all precautions, be prepared to handle a chimney fire in case one does occur. Don't, as a first reaction, pour water into the firebox; there is no surer way to crack a good, cast-iron stove. Do keep a box of table salt or baking soda handy; poured in the firebox, either will help calm the fire while you call the fire department. Dampen down the stove to eliminate the oxygen feeding the fire, open the door to the chimney clean-out and either (1) spray in the contents of a fire extinguisher (see page 9 for fire extinguisher descriptions), or (2) set in a pan of water. The heat will draw up the water which should help quell the flames. Do be sure to shut the chimney clean-out door right away; if it's left open, more air will rush in to feed the fire.

In the event of a stovepipe fire, you may choose just to damp the stove and wait it out; but if it looks more threatening, *carefully* remove the pipe from the stove end and spray in the contents of a fire extinguisher. If the pipe is removed from the flue end, the pull of the draft may cause the fire to flame in your face.

"A big woodpile is as good as having money in the bank."
Leonard Thomas, East Randolph, VT

Stove Storage

If a stove is not going to be used for several weeks or more, remove all traces of ashes and soot and wipe dry the water reservoir. Disconnect the stovepipe from the flue and cover the chimney opening: this will prevent any moisture from getting into the stove and rusting the interior.

If you plan to store the stove in a garage or shed, it will also be necessary to coat the stove's metal with oil, grease or petroleum jelly—anything without salt which retards rust. Don't, however, think of this as a way to recycle old crankcase oil or motor oil because they will do nasty things to your house when the stove is finally re-fired.

GETTING THE FIRE GOING

With the wood range planted safely in the kitchen, and a ready wood or coal supply at hand, it's still more than a simple matter to get the cooking done. You must learn to adjust various grates, drafts, and dampers first to get the fire going, and then to control the flame to produce the kind of heat needed to cook the food. No two stoves are alike; yours will have a personality and quirks of its own—and you will develop your own systems for managing it.

Before building a fire, check to see if there are any pieces of partially burnt wood, clinkers, or an accumulation of ashes. To insure a free-flowing current of air through the firebox— essential for igniting the fire—these should be removed. Save the charred wood for future fires; deposit clinkers and ashes in a metal pail. Before you scatter these outside or store in another container, make sure they're dead: over-hastiness has started more than one fire.

If your stove has a water reservoir, fill it with water before the stove is lit; it should never be allowed to run dry while a fire is going or the heat from the oven may melt the solder as well as, in time, burn out the liner. And if the stove has a hot water front which is attached to a storage tank, it, too, should be filled with water; otherwise it may crack.

Firing Wood

Open wide the draft and damper. This creates a clear passage for air to enter below the fuel, pass through and thereby ignite it, while carrying the gases and smoke out the chimney. The oven damper should be open and the check draft closed.

"You have to learn to run your stove before you can learn to cook."

Perry Wilder, Colrain, MA

Like any good fire, a cookstove fire is built in stages. Remove the cooking lids and T over the firebox and lay in the tinder. I rely upon loosely wadded pages of the Sunday edition of *The New York Times;* as I finish reading one of the sections, that is what starts the fire. (Newspapers from any part of the country, however, will do. Magazines, though, will not; the coated pages admit little air.) Lacking newspapers, use dry leaves, pine needles, milk cartons, cardboard egg cartons, or dried citrus peels—almost anything that is ignitable and dry, but nothing that contains any plastic. Some people soak corncobs in kerosene but kerosene used in any form around fires can be a hazard.

Over the tinder lay, in criss-crossed fashion, several sticks of dry, finely split kindling. Replace the T and back lid and light the tinder from the front. (I keep a box of stick matches tacked to a nearby wall so I don't have to hunt around for them. They're advertised as "strike anywhere" matches, but use the side of the box; if you strike them on the stove, they leave their signature.) Replace the front lid and listen to the fire take off!

If, after a brief flash, you don't hear anything, it means that the kindling is too green or large or that the draft is poor, and the fire has gone out. One method for combatting a cold, slow-starting stove is to burn a few sheets of twisted newspaper in the firebox *before* building the fire. This warms up the stovepipe and chimney flue, helping to create a better draft for igniting the wood.

Once the fire has caught, remove the front lid and add more wood. I never feed a fire through the firebox door; there's too

"Keeping a lid open to see if the fire is catching is irresistible, but it totally spoils the draft."

Gwen Robinson, Orford, NH

great a chance that the ashes and coals may spill and sparks may fly. And to send smoke and ashes billowing up the chimney rather than in your face, open the damper before removing the lid. I add a couple more sticks of softwood until a steady fire is established and then begin adding the hardwood for cooking.

"Keep your firewood covered! If you put a piece covered in ice or snow into the stove, you'll crack the grates."
Charlie Spooner, Bethel, VT

Now the draft/damper adjusting begins! These, apart from the wood, are what control the fire. When both are open, the flames blaze madly, the fire is hot, and the heat escapes. As they are closed, the flames subside, the fire cools, and the heat is retained. You will have to experiment to determine how far each can be closed to permit a steady fire and not cause smoke to pour into the kitchen. By virtue of its design, the damper should allow the smoke a polite exit no matter how far it is closed, but in practice, this is not always so. Flue temperature, chimney height, cleanliness, and the weather all are contributing factors. I always leave mine partially open, anyway, because the flue stays hotter—discouraging creosote—and I needn't worry about errant smoke.

As mentioned, the weather is also a factor in maintaining a hot, smoke-free fire. On clear, breezy, high-pressure system days, everything can be shut down more. On damp, heavy, windless days, the draft and damper will have to be kept open more to create a better draft. If there is a problem with wind blowing down the chimney and smoke puffing back into the room, an extra elbow in the stovepipe may help (it also may reduce the updraft and make it more difficult to start a fire when the stove is cold). For abiding problems with downdrafts, see chapter "Setting Up."

Before the oven damper can be closed for baking and heating the reservoir, the stove and chimney must be sufficiently heated to draw the hot air across and around the oven compartment; if they are too cool, there won't be enough draft and the stove will smoke. If that happens, open the oven damper to release the smoke and open the draft—keeping the stovepipe damper partially closed—to increase the heat. Once there's a steady flame and the beginnings of coals, the oven damper can be closed.

> "Except for starting the fire, I always keep the oven damper closed. This prevents the flames from going up the chimney and igniting any creosote. We had a chimney fire once because the damper was left open. Never again."
>
>   Gladys Dimock, Bethel, VT

Most kinds of cooking require a steady, controlled heat, never an inferno. A stove that is allowed to get overheated— a glowing red cooking surface being a sure-fire sign—can easily warp; especially susceptible are the T's and the lids. To cool a stove, shut the draft, open the check draft, open the damper, and tip the cooking lids. By eliminating the air through the fire and replacing it with cooling air over it, the fire is halted; the tipped lids act as an additional check draft and the opened damper lets the heat escape.

Firing Coal

A coal fire is built much like a wood fire, except that rather than adding cooking wood to the burning kindling, one adds coal. There should be a well-established wood fire covering the entire grate so that the coal, which is added little by little, is evenly ignited. Continue to add more fuel to build up a good bed of coals. If the fire should get particularly low, re-kindle with some wood and add more coal. This makes enough heat to ignite the new coal and prevents the accumulation of un-burned volatile gases.

Unlike cooking with wood, a coal fire must occasionally be cleared of clinkers and ashes to allow more breathing room

"Don't burn coal on a grate meant for wood. In time, you'll burn it out."

Sherry Streeter, Rumson, NJ

for the burning pieces on top. To "shake down" a coal fire, turn the grate bolt crank a quarter or half revolution—enough so that the ashes fall and the larger pieces of burning fuel remain. Never, however, let the ashes accumulate (or in a wood stove, either) to the point that they are nearly level with the bottom of the grate; this will cut off the oxygen feeding the fire and cause the burning coals above to warp, crack, or burn out the grate. Again, a daily removal of ashes is essential for a brisk, well-managed fire.

Banking the Fire

Although its firebox is smaller than that of a heating stove, a wood range, properly banked, may hold a fire overnight. Some stoves, because of the size of the firebox and tightness of construction, will work better than others; coal-burning stoves work best of all.

Wood-burning stoves: To a bed of glowing coals, add the largest piece of unsplit hardwood—preferably a dense, slow-burning wood such as oak, hickory, or black locust—that the firebox will hold. Fit in any smaller sticks, if room permits, and open the draft to ignite the new wood. Now cover everything with ashes; these will help control the fire and retain the heat. Close down the draft to just a crack, open the check draft (experimentation will tell you just how much), and shut down the damper as far as possible without smoking.

Coal-burning stoves: To a bed of glowing coals, add as much coal as the firebox will hold. Check to see that there is not a deep build-up of ashes underneath the grate, shut down the draft and damper—again, leaving them open just enough so that the stove can breathe—and open the check draft. Never close the damper entirely in a coal stove so long as a fire is going because coal gases contain carbon monoxide and if they should escape into the house, the results could be deadly. A banked coal fire should last from twelve to fourteen hours, more than enough time for a good night's rest.

IF THE STOVE SMOKES

* The first fire in a new stove may cause some smoke as the surface oils burn off. This is short-lasting.
* In an old stove, you may have found a previously un-discovered leak. This is not short-lasting and should be fixed.
* The ashbox may need cleaning. A full one will not deliver enough air to feed the fire properly.
* The chimney and stovepipe may need cleaning.
* The horizontal span in the stovepipe may be too long.
* There may be too many elbows in the stovepipe.
* Wait for a change in the weather.
* The flue may not be large enough for the stove.

"Just keep enough wood cut and not try to burn icicles."
Ralph Edson, E. Randolph, VT

OTHER USES OF THE STOVE

For those of us accustomed to using modern stoves, it's difficult to imagine the pivotal position once occupied by the "iron monster" in so many households. Its use transcended that of a cooking appliance and was depended on for far-ranging tasks. In the winter it was what one first headed for upon entering the kitchen: it was a creature to cuddle up to while breakfast was being prepared; and it was a comfort to hand and backsides, fresh from the cold, while the hot chocolate heated. Its warmth lured house pets into spending countless hours snoozing in its grace, and it often drew together the family to share the day's adventures. The fire heated water for the Saturday night bath (a tradition which evolved because of the great effort required to haul water to the house), and the plunge was taken in the barrel tub in front of the open oven. Icy sheets were warmed by bricks, stones, or *freestones* (brick-size pieces of soapstone) that had been heated on top of the stove; as people tucked themselves into bed, they tucked the hot stone into a cloth bag and placed it at their feet.

But not all was rhapsody. On a stuffy summer day, the wood stove was preferably avoided, a pariah to all. Unfortunately, its fever was inescapable for some, as the wash needed boiling and the dried clothes ironing. Great copper boilers and soapstone laundry tubs steamed above the flames and laundresses spent hours fishing out clothes with a long clothes stick. The following passage suggests what wash-days were like before *Maytag* and all-purpose *All:*

Shave thin one-half pound of good hard soap and dissolve in two-thirds boiler of water. Let it come to a boil, then add two and one-half tablespoonfuls of kerosene oil. Dip out some of the hot suds, in which the clothes that are stained or much soiled

may be rubbed slightly before putting into the boiler. Boil briskly from ten to twenty minutes, rub in the suds water if necessary, and rinse as usual. Clothes slightly soiled need not be
rubbed at all before boiling. This is much easier than the old-
fashioned method of washing.

Women's Suffrage Cook Book, 1886

When the wash was removed from the line or clothes rack
(which was sometimes indoors, next to the stove), a collection
of *sad irons*—those cast-iron irons having either a permanent or
interchangeable handle—would be grouped over the firebox; as
the iron in use cooled, it was exchanged for a heated one. Sad
irons—a fitting name—came in one-, two-, and three-pound
weights for pressing different fabric weights, but even so, care
was needed to prevent them from scorching clothes. The iron's
surface was kept clean and smooth by rubbing it with a piece of
wax tied in a cloth and then running it over a cloth or paper
sprinkled with salt.

Some of these practices are outmoded, for which we can be
thankful; others bear no improvement and still are appreciated
today.

Warming Oven

The most frequent uses of the warming oven will be to heat
dinner plates before serving and keep cooked courses warm
while the others are finishing. But its uses extend as far as
your culinary interests and imagination. It's an excellent spot
for raising bread dough and incubating yogurt—but keep the
doors open, as too much heat will kill both the yeast and yogurt
bacteria. Salt stays loose, and wet mittens, scarves and dish

"Keep a loosely covered tin on the shelf to receive all bits of
leftover bread and biscuits for thorough drying, to be fried in
butter for delicious croutons."

Gwen Robinson, Orford, NH

towels get dry. If you raise chickens, keep a tin pan in the warming oven to collect egg shells. Once dried, they make an excellent chicken grit which furnishes them the material for making new shells and keeps them from becoming egg-eaters, which feeding fresh shells may do. In the evening, pour some boiling water over a bowl of dried fruit, stick in the warming oven and enjoy juicy stewed fruit for breakfast. Place the leafy tops of parsley, celery, and onion tops on a drying rack or plate to dry; bottle for later use in soups and stews. Dry papier-maché and modeling clay creations. Anything that profits from a gentle heat will love a warming oven.

Water Reservoir

With a water reservoir, there is always a ready source of hot water for cooking and cleaning. With the cover back, it gives off added humidity to the room; with the cover closed, it's extra space for warming dishes and holding food. If yours is a reservoir that heats to boiling, I've been told it can be used to process canned fruits and vegetables.

Tea Kettle

A cast-iron teakettle humming on the back of the stove is not just a ready source of water for warm drinks, but also a mini-humidifier, sending off a constant column of steam which helps take the crackle out of winter air. It's also a remedy for bouldered brown sugar. Place hardened sugar in a sieve, re-

"Grandma kept several washed eggs in the tea kettle. Instant lunches for hungry kids. If we didn't eat them quickly she fished them out with a slotted spoon and stored them to eat cold or used them in potato salad."

Shirley Sweedman, Max, MN

move the kettle lid, and set the sieve over, but not in, the boiling water. In just a few minutes the sugar will be soft.

If the kettle is continually simmering, it will occasionally need cleaning. Some old-timers kept an oyster shell in the bottom of the kettle—as well as in the reservoir—to prevent fur from forming; others boiled vinegar in it to remove the deposits. And according to the *Home Comfort Cook Book*, "A few stalks of rhubarb cut up and boiled in a teakettle full of water will soften the deposit of lime so that it may all be scraped away."

Wood Ashes

Although they might be considered an inevitable nuisance of wood stove cooking, wood ashes are actually an added bonus. Rich in potash (especially hardwood ashes) and containing smaller amounts of phosphorous, they are excellent for dusting on gardens at the same time other fertilizers are worked into the ground. And their alkalinity sweetens acid soil and pampers lime-loving plants. Wood ashes can be mixed in equal parts with hydrated lime, diluted with water and used as a spray to repel the cucumber beetle, or they can be sprinkled around plants to shield them from slugs.

"Plunging coals into water gives an ample supply of soil-sweetening charcoal for houseplants."
Gwen Robinson, Orford, NH

Lye, a basic ingredient in homemade soap, is made by leaching water through wood ashes (see page 191 for instructions); and as a deodorizer, ashes will improve the atmosphere of a privy if a scoopful is added after each use.

Never store wood ashes where rain can get to them, as water leaches out the potash and destroys their effectiveness.

I store mine in garbage bags all winter long (in the summer I sprinkle them outside). A shovelful scattered over icy pathways makes a non-slip surface, but scrape feet before coming into the house as carpets do not benefit from them. And if your car wheels start spinning on packed snow, throw some ashes under the wheels. That trick has gotten me out of the driveway after many a stormy night.

NOW YOU'RE COOKING

Cookware

Still the most effective for wood stove use is the traditional cast-iron cookware. Many cooks who learned their skills fifty years ago are using the same utensils today. Cast-iron cookware includes many-sized spiders (or skillets), Dutch ovens, bean pots, gem pans, corn cake pans, broilers, and griddles. All are rugged, provide an even heat, and are easy to care for. And the food cooked in them increases in iron content, a benefit to pregnant women and other persons susceptible to anemia.

There are numerous manufacturers of cast-iron cookware, but often the best buys are found in junk shops, at auctions, or garage sales. You even may come across pieces that are no longer made. My most treasured find is a pancake skillet which is composed of three, separate, circular griddles (each the diameter of an orange) hinged lengthwise onto a long, narrow, solid griddle. The batter is poured into the circles, cooked, and then flipped onto the solid griddle. While that side is cooking, the circles are re-filled, making six pancakes cooking at once.

If you acquire any item that is rusted, scrub it with steel wool, wash with soap and water, and dry thoroughly.

Whether old or new, cast iron must be seasoned. Coat the piece with an unsalted oil (vegetable, linseed, suet, lard) and heat in a 300°F. oven for two hours. Apply more oil as it becomes absorbed. When the seasoning is completed, let the utensil cool, and wipe off any excess oil. Repeat when it rusts, or if it causes food to either discolor or acquire a metallic flavor.

Cast iron performs best if it is preheated a minute or so before using. Keep it over a medium to medium-hot heat; for most kinds of cooking, a sizzling hot surface is unnecessary.

I know one cook who has been using the same skillet for the forty years she has been cooking over wood, and she vows soap has never sudsed its surface. She either rubs out any tidbits and grease with paper towels, or scrapes it clean with a spatula, or scours the pan with salt. This prevents the formation of rust and helps to preserve the seasoning. For really tough, encrusted remains, soak the utensil in water all night and scrape clean in the morning.

"If you never scour with soap or detergents, pans become a little like Teflon."

Gladys Dimock, Bethel, VT

Heavy enamelware also works well on wood stoves, but is more of a problem to keep clean (if such things matter). Copper-bottomed pots are dreary for this reason, which further buttresses the practicality of cast iron, since it gradually and naturally takes on a lovely shade of black.

A *wok,* the Chinese deep-dished basin which was designed to fit in a brazier over a bed of coals, is equally at home on a kitchen range. Select a heavy-grade wok, as it will heat more evenly and hold up longer. Like cast-iron cookware, a wok also must be seasoned. A new wok first should be scrubbed both inside and out with soap and water to remove the anti-rust coating. After it is rinsed and dried, rub the inside with peanut, corn, or soybean oil and slowly heat until the oil smokes. After several minutes, remove the wok from the heat and let it cool. Wipe off any excess oil and the wok is ready for use.

Also like cast iron, a wok doesn't benefit from soap. After each use, rinse in water, dry, and rub a few drops of oil over the surface to prevent it from rusting. For really cooked-on messes, professional Chinese cooks merely heat the wok until the residue burns off.

Soapstone, a granite-like rock which is quite soft and greasy feeling (hence the name), has long been recognized for its heat-absorbing properties, and has been used for facing heating stoves since the late 1700's. It's also an excellent material for cooking as it heats evenly, and the smooth surface rarely needs greasing. Washing is also unnecessary. Just wipe with a damp cloth or, for stubborn spots, rub with salt and a coarse cloth. A twelve-inch griddle is available from the Vermont Soapstone Co., Perkinsville, VT 05151, and according to that company, "The more the griddle is used, the better it works!"

Ceramic and earthenware pots can be used on the top of the stove as well as in the oven. They must, however, be exposed to the heat gradually, as clay, unlike metal, will not tolerate sudden jumps in temperature. Romertompf pots are excellent roasters. A friend of mine, who is the mother of four and partner in her husband's business, often sticks in a potful of food in the morning and comes back at the end of the day to a cooked dinner. (Her stove is fueled by coal and easily will hold a fire all day.) She insists the taste is superior to anything stewed in a crock pot.

Although some cookware works better than others, any will do. However, if yours is equipped with plastic or wooden handles, take caution, as close proximity to intense heat does neither material any good. Also, don't be careless about leaving rubber spatulas and plastic dishware or utensils on the stove: not only might they melt to uselessness, but it's nearly impossible to unglue them from the stove. And by all means, keep potholders handy! A wood cookstove heats the entire cooking vessel, and what is safe to handle on other ranges will raise blisters on this.

A neat little item which can be installed in the stovepipe of your kitchen range or heating stove is a stovepipe drum oven. It is equipped with a thermometer on the door, an oven rack, and a soot cleaner; and not only is it good for baking, but, with its door left open, it throws off additional heat into the room. Order from Louisville Tin and Stove Co., P.O. Box 1079, Louisville, KY 40201.

Top-of-the-Stove Cooking

Think of a wood cookstove as you would any other, except that rather than pushing buttons, you'll be pushing pots. It equally provides a blazing hot fire for Chinese stir-frying and rapid boils, a hot fire for deep-fat frying, a moderate heat for sautéeing, and a slow, steady heat for "crock pot" style cooking—and all at the same time. Pots can be moved from one kind of heat to another—as cooking often demands—and the reaction is immediate. There is no waiting for a glowing red electric burner to cool to low, and gone is the annoyance of turning down a gas burner so far that the flame goes out. Also, the large heated stove top encourages the use of any size pan with the assurance that its entire bottom will heat evenly.

Because stoves differ—as will the location of the flame in the same stove—there is no hard and fast rule for declaring which cooking lid is the hottest or coolest. Generally, however, the hottest lid is that which sits over the back of the firebox, and the hottest area lies between it and the stovepipe. The coolest lids are those on the side opposite the firebox. The mid-range lids are cool when the fire first starts, but as the stove heats—especially after closing the oven damper—they will be almost as hot as the lids over the firebox. Many stoves are equipped with one lid composed of three, removable, concentric rings. This allows any size pan to sit directly over the fire when an intense cooking heat is required. And if the stove top gets too hot for your cooking needs, set the pan on either a metal trivet, a couple of bricks, or any heat-resistant item which lifts the pan off the stove.

Wok Cooking

For stir-frying, the food should be uniformly and thinly sliced. The heat should be intense so that the food cooks quickly; this helps preserve the nutrients and seal in the flavors. Remove

one of the lids over the firebox and set in the wok. Pre-heat to a high temperature, add the oil, and begin cooking immediately; if the oil is pre-heated too much, the food may stick.

Traditionally the vegetables, or complements, are cooked before the meat, or principal. Cook and stir the vegetables until crispy and almost done, and then push them to the upper sides of the wok, away from the heat, or remove and keep warm. Re-heat wok, add more oil, and add the principal. When three-quarters done, return the complement, and stir and cook until done—which is usually no more than a minute or so.

A wok also may be used for deep-fat frying, steaming, making omelettes, and simmering soups. For moderate cooking heats, place the wok on its metal ring, either above a removed lid or on the stove's surface. The kind of cooking will determine where it sits, and there seems to be no end to the kinds it can do.

Broiling

Of primary importance for successful broiling is a good body of coals. They should be an iridescent red, glowing rather than flaming, and uniformly distributed. If any gray spots occur, rake the coals so that the food will cook evenly.

On most stoves, there are two different ways to broil. One is to remove the lids and T above the firebox and either lay across a flat, wire grill (I use the oven rack from an old gas oven), or hold a long-handled, hinged, campfire style broiler

"Broiling is cooking over or in front of a clear fire. The food to be cooked is usually placed in a greased broiler or on a gridiron held near the coals, turned often at first to sear the outside—thus preventing escape of inner juices—afterwards turned occasionally."

The Boston Cooking-School Cook Book, 1896

over the coals. The second method is to insert the long-stemmed broiler through the check draft door. Both require that the draft and damper be kept partially open so that the coals glow and the smoke retreats up the chimney. In the beginning you may want to hold the food close to the coals; by quickly searing the outside, the juices are sealed in. Afterwards, raise the food, but turn it often so that any juices that do escape head back into the meat rather than onto the fire. You will find, as I have, that no special turn in the weather is necessary to enjoy a barbecue because you've already got the makings right in your kitchen.

Baking and Roasting

Using the oven successfully is the greatest challenge of wood stove cookery. Not only is it a matter of juggling drafts, dampers, doors, lids, and size and kinds of fuel wood, but also it involves gauging such intangibles as the feel, smell, and appearance of the food you're cooking.

Once the oven damper is shut, most ovens take about thirty to forty minutes to heat to 350°F., so plan ahead. Though many cookstoves are equipped with a thermometer on the oven door, many are not. If yours is without such a convenience,

"Don't be afraid to try again if you fail again and again; success is the result of perseverance and application."

Home Comfort Cook Book

don't feel deprived, because it's unusual for those that do—at least for older stoves—to work properly. Below is how our predecessors reckoned temperature:

> "To ascertain the right heat of the oven, put a piece of writing paper into it, and if it is a chocolate brown in five minutes it is the right heat for biscuits, muffins, and small pastry. It is called a quick oven. If the paper is dark yellow it is the right heat for bread, pound cake, puddings and puff paste pies. When the paper is light yellow it is right for sponge cake."
>
> *Domestic Cookbook* 1888

> "Many test their ovens this way: If the hand can be held in 20-25 seconds, it is a 'quick oven,' 35-45 seconds is 'moderate,' and 45-60 seconds is 'slow.' All systematic housekeepers will hail the day when some enterprising Yankee or Buckeye girl shall invent a stove or range with a thermometer attached to the oven, so that the heat may be regulated accurately and intelligently."
>
> *Practical Housekeeper*, 1884

Many experienced cooks calculate temperature by very briefly sticking their hands in the oven; others know by the feel of the door. A functioning door thermometer registers the temperature of the middle of the oven, but lacking this, the same results are achieved by purchasing a portable oven thermometer and placing it inside on the middle of the rack. For all recipes in this book, a slow oven is 250°–325°F., moderate 325°–400°F., and fast 400°–500°F.

This much accomplished, it still may be necessary to get to know the "hot spots" in your oven. The side next to the firebox is often hotter than the farther side, and the upper half—because a wood stove heats from the top down—hotter than the lower. An easy way to determine how the different areas in an oven vary in temperature is to bake a large sheet of biscuits, following the directions for temperature and time. After the biscuits are removed you can judge where the heat is most and least intense by the brownness of their crusts. You may find that rotating the food, every so often, will be vital for even cooking.

If there is a problem with tops of food browning too fast, try cooking on the floor of the oven rather than on the rack.

Other tricks include covering the food with a pan, a sheet of foil, or a piece of wet or greased brown paper. There are also new heat-tolerant plastic bags which allow the food to cook but prevent it from burning. When roasting, enclose the pan and all, and you'll have the juices swimming in the roaster rather than sloshing around in the bag.

There are some foods, however, which profit from an initial high heat. Fancily shaped bread doughs preserve their shape by a quick-forming crust, and roasts and poultry retain their juices. Afterwards they should be baked or roasted at a lower temperature or on a lower level.

To brown the tops of food, move the food near the top of the oven, increase the fire by adding finely split pieces of wood, and open the draft. If this fails, the oven needs cleaning.

There are as many ways to manage an oven as there are cooks to tell about it, so I will merely give what works for me. I find it easier to bake with coals rather than with flames— the oven temperature is no longer building and there is less chance that the goods will burn. For short baking times (up to an hour), a bed of glowing coals will maintain the heat long enough without needing more wood. The draft is opened a crack, and the damper closed. For longer periods, I add un-split hardwood sticks, one at a time, to the bed of coals. Too large a stick will cool the fire, and too small a stick will add a sudden burst of heat. Again, it just takes practice.

But maintaining a perfectly steady temperature is, at best, unreasonable. There are, however, a few measures which do provide some control. If the oven gets too cool, open the draft and add split sticks of dry hardwood until the desired tempera-ture is reached. If the oven gets too hot, there's a choice of techniques. The most immediate is to open the oven door, but if a more gradual heat reduction is wanted, (a) partially open the oven damper and close the draft, or (b) tilt open the lids over the oven, or (c) open the check draft, or (d) place a pan of cold water in the oven and re-fill as needed until the tempera-ture has dropped.

Most of the recipes in this book call for fixed cooking times, but take these more as hints rather than commandments. There is too much irregularity in oven temperature to predict accurately how much time is needed: hot ovens cook food faster, and cool ovens slower. Sometimes, it's just as simple as that.

Canning

On the positive side, wood stove canning is economically more attractive than using either electricity or gas. The long cooking times required for both the preparation of some foods and the processing of most recommend an energy-saving fuel source. (The flavor of two-day-simmered tomato sauce is unsurpassed!) Also, large containers—such as old copper tubs—can be used for the boiling water bath method as the entire bottom heats sufficiently to bring the contents to a rolling boil. And the larger the container, the more jars that can be processed at once.

But let us consider the drawbacks. Constant attention is demanded because the water must be kept boiling. When using a pressure canner, a steady steam pressure must be maintained; fluctuations in temperature may cause a loss of liquid from the jars. Once the required pressure is reached, you may have to move the canner to a cooler lid to keep it from building. And be sure to keep the fire stoked, for if the pressure drops below the recommended poundage, you may have to start the whole process over again. Once the processing time is up, remove the canner from the stove.

Apart from such vigilance, the only other hassle may be one's reluctance to slave over a hot stove during the height of summer (this must be the source of that expression). Summer kitchens obviate this discomfort, but if you're in a small, enclosed area, there's no blame for turning on the electricity or gas. In fact, it's times like these when a combination wood/ gas or wood/electricity stove is particularly rewarding.

If you're unfamiliar with proper canning methods, don't take chances by proceeding simply on recollections of mother or the advice of friends. Read a book which fully describes the necessary steps and your hard-earned produce will keep safer and longer.

Drying

For conserving space and energy, drying is the most practical method for preserving food, and, except for the sun, a wood range is the most economical means for doing it. I will not attempt to explain all the necessary steps for drying food—the blanching, sulphuring, and use of anti-oxidants—as that is a science in itself; instead, I will show just how to use the stove for this most ancient way of preserving food.

The oven is one way to do it. Spread prepared food on wooden frames covered with coarse cotton cloth and set trays in the center of the oven—lower rather than higher—where a more moderate and stable heat can be more easily maintained. The oven temperature should not exceed 150°F. and so careful attention is necessary to avoid fluctuations. Set a thermometer on an upper oven rack to monitor the temperature; if it climbs too high, open the oven door. Once the proper drying heat is regained, the lids over the oven may have to be tipped to keep the temperature from climbing.

Begin with an old, banked fire with plenty of coals. Add only one stick of wood at a time, and keep the draft and damper almost closed. The check draft may have to be opened to govern the fire.

A seventy-eight-year-old friend of mine recalls his mother hanging mesh trays from the ceiling near the stove which she covered with pumpkin and apple chunks. The rising heat was sufficient to dry the food. Some foods, like apple slices and string beans, can be strung on a thread and hung, clothesline style, above or behind the stove.

The warming oven is also a handy place for drying. Again, though, take care with the temperature—too cool a temperature means a longer drying time, and if too hot, the food may cook and more vitamins will be lost. By opening and closing the warming oven doors, the heat can be controlled.

To dry food on top of the stove, a special device is needed. The accompanying diagram is for a dryer box that you can make yourself.

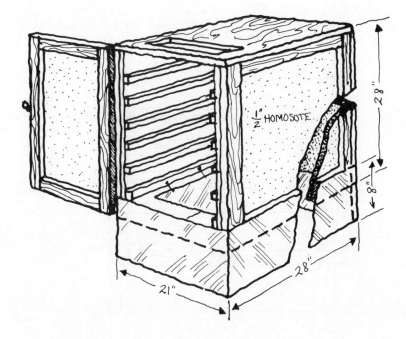

The side frames are made from one-inch by four-inch wood covered with homasote (a ½-inch-thick insulated building board); the tray supports are ¾- x ¾-inch wood; the top and back are of ½-inch plywood; the base and baffle are cut from heavy sheet metal; the hinged door can either be a frame made from one-inch by four-inch wood covered with homasote, or a solid piece of ½-inch plywood; and the trays are frames made from ¾- x ¾-inch wood covered with coarse cotton cloth. Follow the diagram for dimensions and spacing.

1. Nail or screw together the two side frames.
2. From the inside, nail on homasote to frames.
3. Nail or screw tray supports to side frames.
4. Add screw eyes to bottom tray supports to hold metal baffle.
5. Cut air vent in plywood top of dryer box.
6. Nail or screw framed sides to plywood back.
7. Nail or screw top of dryer box to sides and back.
8. Screw on sheet metal base to bottom of dryer box.

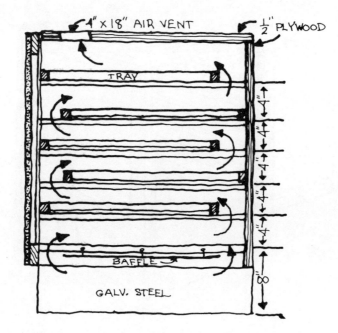

9. Add hinged door and attach a small latch.
10. Install 17-inch x 24-inch sheet metal baffle, suspending it with wire from the screw eyes.
11. Make drying tray frames a little narrower than the inside dimensions (for easy sliding) and 4 inches shorter. Tack on cloth or staple to the sides of the tray.

The trays should be staggered on the tray supports so that one is pushed forward and the next pushed back; this channels the warm air so that the food dries evenly. Place food on the trays and set the dryer box over the cooler side of the stove. Again, watch the temperature and move or elevate the dryer box if temperature adjustments are necessary.

RECIPES

This is a collection of some of my favorite recipes and those of correspondents and friends. To all of you who helped me, I offer warm-hearted thanks.

Also included are a number of family treasures—which have been handed down from one generation to the next—and some old "receipts" found in cookbooks written when people cooked only on wood- or coal-fueled stoves. Some of these may appeal only to a sense of history; others may inspire some old-fashioned cooking.

As familiarity with the wood stove grows, so does the confidence that anything cooked on a "turn-on" stove is adaptable to a wood range. The only obstacle is an unwillingness to try.

BREAKFASTS

PANCAKES

Set a heavy skillet or griddle over medium-hot heat and wait until a few drops of cold water sprinkled on the surface bounce and then disappear. If the water evaporates before the bounce, the skillet is too hot and should be moved to a cooler spot. The skillet also may become too hot during cooking, so be watchful for burnt bottoms.

Snow Griddle Cakes

Take six tablespoonfuls flour, add a little salt, and six table-spoonfuls of light, fresh-fallen snow. Stir the flour and snow well together, adding a pint of sweet milk. Bake the batter in small cakes on a griddle, using only a very little butter. They may be eaten with butter and sugar, and are very delicate.

The Woman's Suffrage Cook-Book, 1888

Basic Pancake Batter   Serves 4

1½ cups wholewheat or
    unbleached white flour
½ tsp. salt
2 tsp. baking soda
1½ cups milk, sweet, sour
    or buttermilk
1 tsp. honey, molasses, or
    sugar
2 eggs, slightly beaten
3 Tbsp. oil

Tasty Additions:

1 cup blueberries or
    sliced strawberries
1 apple, chopped, and
    1 tsp. cinnamon
1 cup chocolate chips
1 cup nuts, chopped
½ cup wheat berry or
    alfalfa sprouts
½ cup shredded coconut
    and ½ cup pineapple
    bits

In a mixing bowl, combine the flour, salt and baking soda. Add milk, sweetener, eggs and oil; stir until dry ingredients are moistened. For a Tasty Addition, add it now. Drop batter by large spoonfuls onto skillet.

Best Banana Pancakes Serves 4

1 cup flour
½ cup wheat germ
2 tsp. baking soda
1 tsp. salt
1 cup milk

2 eggs, slightly beaten
3 Tbsp. oil
2 very ripe bananas,
mashed

In a mixing bowl, combine the flour, wheat germ, baking soda and salt. In a separate bowl, combine the milk, eggs, oil and bananas; beat until well mixed. Add liquid ingredients to dry ingredients and stir just until blended. Drop by large spoonfuls onto skillet.

T.J. Goetting, Odessa, DE

Buckwheat Pancakes Serves 4

2 tsp. dry yeast
2 cups milk, scalded and
cooled to lukewarm
2 cups buckwheat flour
½ tsp. salt
2 Tbsp. molasses

½ tsp. baking soda,
dissolved in ¼ cup
lukewarm water
1 egg
¼ cup oil

In a mixing bowl, combine yeast and milk, stirring to dissolve. Stir in flour and salt until mixture is smooth. Cover with a cloth and let stand at room temperature overnight. Before cooking, stir in molasses, baking soda, egg and oil. Grease skillet lightly and spoon on batter.

Don't throw away leftover batter: make into pancakes or waffles, freeze, and toast for a quick breakfast.

Pumpkin Indian Cakes

Take equal portions of Indian meal, and stewed pumpkin that has been well mashed and drained very dry in a sieve or cullender. Put the stewed pumpkin into a pan, and stir the meal gradually into it, a spoonful at a time, adding a little butter as you proceed. Mix the whole thoroughly, stirring it very hard. If not thick enough to form a stiff dough, add a little more Indian meal. Make it into round, flat cakes, about the size of a muffin, and bake them over the fire on a hot griddle greased with butter. Or lay them in a square iron pan, and bake them in an oven.

Miss Leslie's New Receipts for Cooking, 1850

Canadian Sour Cream Pancakes   Serves 4

1 cup sour cream
2 cups flour
1 Tbsp. honey or molasses

1 tsp. baking soda
1 tsp. salt
1 or 2 eggs, beaten

In a pitcher, combine the sour cream, flour, sweetener and baking soda. Cover with a cloth, put in a warm spot—like the warming oven—and let stand overnight. In the morning, add salt and enough eggs to give it pouring consistency. Stir well and pour pancakes onto a well-greased, hot griddle.

Paula Olson, Ontario, Canada

Cottage Cheese Pancakes   Serves 4

6 eggs, separated	1 tsp. salt
2 cups cottage cheese, small curd	½ tsp. cinnamon
2/3 cup flour	1 tsp. vanilla
2 Tbsp. honey	1 tsp. grated lemon peel

Blend together egg yolks, cottage cheese, flour, honey, salt, cinnamon, vanilla and lemon peel. An electric mixer works best for this. Fold in stiffly beaten egg whites. Drop by spoonful onto a hot griddle. These are delicious with maple syrup, confectioners' sugar and lemon juice, or apple butter.

Corn Crispy-Crunchies   Serves 2-3

1 cup milk	1 cup corn meal
2 eggs	1 tsp. salt
1 Tbsp. honey	½ cup peanuts, chopped
3 Tbsp. oil	

In a mixing bowl, beat together milk, eggs, honey and oil. Add corn meal, salt and peanuts; stir until moistened. Drop onto skillet by large spoonfuls.

Sour Dough Pancakes Serves 4

1 cake or package yeast
2 cups warm water
2 cups flour
½ tsp. salt

1 egg, beaten
1 tsp. baking soda
2 Tbsp. oil
1 Tbsp. honey

Dissolve yeast in warm water and stir in flour. Set in a warm place overnight, like the warming oven or cooling-down stove. Before cooking, measure out ½ cup of this starter, put in a scalded jar, and store in refrigerator for future pancakes, muffins or biscuits. Mix starter with remaining ingredients and add a little milk if batter is too thick. Drop onto a hot skillet.

Walter Goodridge, Conway, MA

Sunday Morning Special

3 cups flour
6 eggs, well beaten
2 Tbsp. brandy
1 tsp. salt

1 tsp. grated orange peel
1 tsp. grated lemon peel
Milk, about 3 cups

Combine all ingredients and add just enough milk to give it a thinnish consistency. Pour to cover a well-buttered nine-inch frying pan. Brown both sides, roll up, and cover with powdered sugar. Makes about 6-8 pancakes.

Fran Ferriss, East Hampton, NY

FRITTERS

Apple Slaps   Serves 3-4

1/3 cup flour
¼ cup wheat germ
1 tsp. baking soda
½ tsp. salt
½ tsp. cinnamon
½ cup milk

1 egg, beaten
1½ Tbsp. oil
3 large apples (about),
   cored and sliced
Butter

In a mixing bowl, combine flour, wheat germ, baking soda, salt and cinnamon. Stir in milk, egg and oil until dry ingredients are just moistened. Dip apple slices in batter and fry on a hot skillet, greased with lots of butter.

Venetian Fritters

3 ounces whole rice
1 pint milk
2 ounces sugar
1 ounce butter
Grated rind of ½ lemon

3 ounces currants
4 ounces minced apple
1 tsp. flour
A little salt
3 eggs

Put rice in cold milk; bring to a slow boil, stirring often and let it simmer until thick and dry. When about three parts done, add sugar, butter, one grain salt, lemon. Let it cool until just warm. Add currants, apples, flour and eggs. Drop the mixture into small fritters, fry them in butter from five to seven minutes, and let them become quite firm on one side before they are turned.

Mrs. Hale's New Cookbook, 1873

Summer Squash Fritters

4-5 small yellow squash,   ½ tsp. salt
   grated   ½ tsp. cinnamon
  3 eggs, beaten   ¼ tsp. allspice
  4 Tbsp. flour

Combine all ingredients. Drop batter onto a hot, buttered skillet and cook until brown. Serve with maple syrup.

WAFFLES

Non-electric waffle irons come in a variety of designs and metals, but basically, they're all used the same way. Grease the two halves and set waffle iron over the hottest lid. When the bottom half is very hot—indicated when drops of water sprinkled on the surface sizzle and steam—turn the iron over and heat the second half to the same temperature. Just before baking, turn waffle iron so that the hot side is on top and pour in the batter, adding only enough to cover about the middle two-thirds of the surface; when the halves are closed, the batter will be pressed out to the sides. Bake a minute on each side, continuing to cook and turn until steam is no longer puffing out the seam. After removing the cooked waffle, flip the waffle iron over and add more batter.

Light-Weight Waffles   Serves 4

2 cups flour
1 tsp. baking soda
½ tsp. salt
2 eggs, separated

2 cups milk, sour or
  buttermilk
1 cup oil

Sift dry ingredients into mixing bowl. Stir in egg yolks, milk, and oil. Fold in stiffly beaten egg whites. For interest, add any or all or a combination of the following: ham bits, bacon bits, walnuts or pecans, diced bananas, shredded coconut, or berries.

Paul's Waffles   Serves 2-3

1½ cups unbleached white
    flour
 3 tsp. baking powder
 ½ tsp. salt

6 Tbsp. melted butter
1 cup milk
3 eggs, separated
1 Tbsp. sugar

Beat egg whites until stiff. Combine rest of ingredients in another bowl and stir only until moistened. Fold in egg whites.
                    Paul Falcone, East Randolph, VT

Sour Cream Waffles   Serves 2-3

1 cup whole wheat pastry
  flour
2 tsp. baking powder
¼ tsp. salt
1 tsp. baking soda

1 Tbsp. honey
3 eggs, separated
2 cups sour cream
1 tsp. grated orange or
  lemon peel

Sift dry ingredients into mixing bowl. Stir in honey, egg yolks, sour cream and citrus peel. Fold in stiffly beaten egg whites.
                    Walter Goodridge, Conway, MA

Corny Yogurt Waffles   Serves 4

1 cup flour	4 eggs, separated
3 tsp. baking powder	2 cups yogurt
1 tsp. baking soda	1 cup melted butter,
½ tsp. salt	cooled
1 cup yellow corn meal	

Sift together flour, baking powder, soda and salt. Add corn meal. In separate bowl, beat egg yolks, yogurt and melted butter. Combine liquid and dry ingredients until just moistened. Fold in stiffly beaten egg whites.

COOKED CEREALS

Delicious cereals can be made from whole grains and water; set the pot on the back of the stove or in the oven at night, and breakfast will be waiting the next morning. This is the way many a farm family would start the day. If you have your own grinder, all the better. The grains will be fresher, thus better tasting and with higher nutritional value.

Ground Grain Cereal

To one cup of ground grains (steel-cut oats, rolled oats, corn meal, brown rice, grits, millet, soy grits, rye grits, buckwheat grits, wheat grits) add two to four cups of cold water and a half teaspoon salt. Bring water to a boil, stir, and cook for about three minutes. Move pot so that water slowly simmers and cook twenty minutes more. If preparing the night before, push pot to the back of the stove or set in the oven. The heavier the pot, such as cast-iron or earthenware, the better it will retain heat.

Mixed Crunch

2/3 cup cracked wholewheat   1 Tbsp. sunflower seeds,
1/3 cup rolled oats   hulled
                                               2½ cups cold water

Put ingredients in a saucepan, bring water to a boil, push pan
to the back of the stove and let sit overnight. Serve with
honey, fruit, wheat germ, or whatever sounds good.

Corn Meal Mush

1 cup stone-ground corn   1 tsp. salt
    meal   4 cups boiling water
1 cup cold water

Mix together corn meal, cold water, and salt. Place boiling
water in the top of a double boiler and add other ingredients.
Cook and stir for three minutes over hottest part of the fire,
then move to more moderate heat and let it steam for fifteen
minutes. Stir frequently and serve.

"Anyone will love corn meal mush if it is baked all night. While
the girls were doing the supper dishes, I would mix corn meal
mush according to directions on the package and remove it from
the heat as soon as all the lumps were out and before it had a
chance to thicken. I poured it into a clean covered bean pot, put
the pot in the oven and left it there all night. We used to night-
fire the cookstove and in the morning after the fire was mended,
I simply reached into the oven for a hot, nourishing breakfast."
Shirley Sweedman, Max, MN

Oatmeal and Apples

1 cup rolled oats   2 tart apples, grated
2 cups cold water   ½ tsp. cinnamon
½ tsp. salt

Combine oats and water and bring to a boil. Cover pan and let
slowly simmer about ten minutes. Add apple and cinnamon,
stir into oatmeal, cover and let cook ten minutes more. This is
also good cooked overnight. Serve with honey and milk.

SOUPS AND STEWS

The advantage of cooking soups and stews on a wood range is that the pot can be set at the back of the stove to simmer for hours, a method recognized for improving the flavor and tenderness of foods. And the aromas from this gentle cooking will enrich the warmth of your home.

"Most of the food was cooked on the back of the stove all day, like a crock pot does today."

Georgene Goetting, Beaver Dam, WI

SOUPS

Classic Black Bean Soup   Serves 8-10

2 cups black beans
8 cups cold water
2 stalks celery, chopped
2 medium onions,
  chopped
¼ cup butter
1 ham bone
¼ cup parsley, chopped
2 bay leaves

½ tsp. salt
¼ tsp. freshly ground
  pepper
½ cup dry sherry
2 thin-skinned lemons,
  sliced thin
2 hard-cooked eggs, sliced
  thin

Soak beans overnight and discard any that float. Drain, put beans in a large kettle, and cover with cold water. Cover kettle and simmer for about one and a half hours, or until tender. Sauté celery and onions in butter until onions are transparent. Add to beans with ham bone, parsley, bay leaves, salt and pepper. Cover and simmer three more hours. Remove ham bone and purée soup in a blender or food mill. Add sherry, and reheat. Serve topped with lemon and egg slices.

Judy Streeter, Madison, CT

Stock

It is simple to extract the juices of meats and bones by long and gentle simmering. A shank or other meat bones, the carcass of a roast turkey or chicken, the trimmings of roasts or steaks are all excellent to prepare stock from. Put in a pot and cover with cold water, add a handful of salt and boil gently for several hours. Do not add any vegetables or spices as all vegetables lose their freshness and flavor by long continued cooking and the flavor of the spice might conflict with the other ingredients of the soup for which the stock is intended. Skim off all scum that rises and add water from time to time as the stock boils away. When you are ready to make the soup, take out all the meat and bones and strain the stock through a sieve, a hair one if you have it; the stock is now ready for use unless you want a perfectly clear soup. In that case, after the stock is strained, put it back in the pot and stir in one or more beaten eggs; put back on the fire and as it boils up the egg will rise; skim off and strain again and your stock will be clear. If you have more than you need for immediate use, put aside in a stone or earthen jar; it will keep for several days in a cold place.

The Century Cook Book, 1894

Pot-au-Feu

In the winter time, our soup kettle went more or less constantly. It started with a few beef bones in a large kettle. Then all the leftovers and pot "lickers" are added as time goes on along with an occasional small handful of washed white or wild rice or pearl barley. After the first day of cooking, the kids help themselves whenever the notion strikes. After every meal all the bones, whether turkey, chicken, duck, beef, pork chop bones, etc., are added to the kettle. One day I add tomatoes and the next time hot water. Each day the soup must be tasted and seasoned accordingly. About every three or four days the kettle must be dumped of bones and a new kettle of soup started. Sometimes the kids will dip to the bottom of the kettle taking out a share of the bones along with their plate of soup, if they particularly like the day's version. If they keep enough of the bones picked out I won't dump the soup kettle quite so quickly. You need not worry about the soup souring as long as you keep fire in the stove. Believe it or not, the more it is cooked, the tastier it gets.

Shirley Sweedman, Max, MN

Piccalilli Soup

1 onion, chopped
1 large clove garlic,
   minced
1 package yellow peas,
   washed
3 chicken bouillon cubes
Salt and pepper
Tabasco sauce
Summer savory

1 bay leaf
1 tsp. cinnamon
Tomato purée
2 generous Tbsp. red
   piccalilli
1 cup chopped cooked
   carrots and their juice
1 cup green beans
Yellow corn

Sauté onion with garlic. Add peas, sauté a little, and sprinkle with powdered bouillon cubes. Pour in enough hot water or stock to make servings, and season with salt and pepper, Tabasco, summer savory, bay leaf, and cinnamon. Cook on back of stove one hour. Put all through blender and add tomato purée until it's a good color. Add piccalilli, carrots, green beans, and enough yellow corn to add interest. Simmer until suppertime.

Gwen Robinson, Orford, NH

Soup for an Invalid

Cut in small pieces one pound of beef or mutton, or part of both; boil it gently in two quarts of water; take off the scum, and when reduced to a pint, strain it. Season with a little salt, and take a teacupful at a time.

Mrs. Hale's New Cookbook, 1873

If soup is too salty, add slices of raw potatoes and boil a few minutes until saltiness is reduced to taste.

Captain's Fish Chowder

2 slices bacon
1 onion, diced
3 medium-sized potatoes
1 carrot, diced
2 cups hot water

1 lb. fillet of cod or
  haddock, cut into 2-inch
  pieces
2 cups milk
1 tsp. salt
½ tsp. paprika

Cook bacon, remove from pan, and cook onion in bacon fat. Add potatoes, carrot, and water. Cover and boil about five minutes. Add fish to vegetables, cover, and simmer for ten minutes. Add milk and salt. Heat just to boiling. Move to lower heat and cook five minutes more. Crumble the bacon and add to chowder just before serving.

Louise Silloway, Randolph Center, VT

Home-Grown Tomato Soup

A fast, delicious soup for those surplus tomatoes.

1 large onion, chopped
1 clove garlic, minced
2 Tbsp. butter
About 7 tomatoes, peeled
  and chopped
3 Tbsp. raw rice
½ tsp. sugar

2 tsp. cumin
½ tsp. chili powder
Salt and pepper to taste
1½ cups garbanzo beans,
  cooked and ½ cup broth
  or 1 14 oz. can garbanzo
  beans with juice
½ tsp. sugar

Sauté onions and garlic in butter until just limp. Place them with tomatoes, rice, sugar, and spices in a kettle and simmer twenty minutes. Add garbanzo beans and heat another three minutes.

Shirley Goetting, New Haven, CT

Zucchini Summer Soup   Serves 4

Traditionally this soup is served cold, but it's equally good piping hot.

5 or 6 small zucchini, washed	1 cup heavy cream
1 large onion, thinly sliced	½ cup milk
1½ tsp. curry powder	Salt and freshly ground
3 cups chicken broth	pepper
	Finely chopped chives

Trim ends off zucchini. Slice one zucchini in two, and cut one of the halves in match-like strips. Bring a small saucepan of water to a boil and add the strips; boil until just tender. Drain and set aside. Cut the remaining half and the rest of the zucchini into one inch lengths; quarter each length. Place the zucchini pieces in a heavy pot, add the onions, and sprinkle on curry powder. Add the chicken broth and bring to a boil. Cover, push pot to the far side, and simmer for about forty-five minutes. Remove soup and put through a blender or food mill to make a purée. Return soup to the pot and add cream, milk, salt and pepper. To serve hot, heat soup, but do not boil. To serve cold, refrigerate until thoroughly chilled. Serve topped with zucchini strips and chives.

Canadian Pea Soup

3 cups whole dried peas	1 diced stalk of celery
½ pound salt pork	8 small new potatoes
2 diced onions	Salt and pepper to taste

Soak peas overnight. Place in kettle with four quarts of water. Add salt pork and vegetables. Cook for two and one-half hours, slowly. Add small, new potatoes and cook for one-half hour longer—or until potatoes are done. This is exceptionally tasty.

Carolyn T. Kelley, Camden, ME

Scalloped Potato Soup

The day before, bake enough scalloped potatoes to have left-overs. Put in blender, adding enough cream and milk for desired servings. If too thin, add more boiled, puréed potatoes. Excellent as is with croutons, or a superb base for chowders.

Gwen Robinson, Orford, NH

Garlic Croutons: For every 1½ cups of dried bread crumbs, slightly crush two cloves garlic. Heat four Tbsp. butter in heavy skillet, and add garlic and bread crumbs. Cook and stir until cubes are brown all over. Drain cubes and discard garlic.

Lentil Soup

1 quart chicken or meat stock
1 cup lentils, washed
2 tomatoes, peeled and quartered
1 clove garlic, minced
1 large onion, chopped
1 bay leaf
6 peppercorns, ground
Worcestershire sauce
Tabasco sauce
2 stalks celery with leaves, chopped
3 medium carrots, chopped
1 tsp. dill or caraway seeds
½ lb. spinach, washed and stemmed
Plain yogurt, optional

In a Dutch oven or other large pot, combine stock, lentils, tomatoes, garlic, onion, bay leaf, peppercorns, Worcestershire sauce and Tabasco. Cook over medium-low heat until lentils are tender (about one hour). Add celery, carrots, and dill or caraway seeds. Cook until vegetables are almost tender. Add spinach and cook ten minutes more. Add more broth, water or tomato juice if liquid gets too low. Serve with a dollop of yogurt.

Vivian's Delicious Vegetable-Beef Soup

1 meaty beef shank
2 quarts cold water
2 medium onions, chopped
1 cup celery, sliced
1 cup peas
1 cup green beans, sliced
1 cup carrots, sliced
3 medium potatoes, in chunks

1 16 oz. can tomatoes
1 green pepper, chopped
1 cup okra, optional
1 Tbsp. Worcestershire sauce
2 beef bouillon cubes
4 peppercorns
Spaghetti

Cover shank with cold water, bring to a boil, and cook fifteen minutes. Remove scum. Add rest of ingredients and simmer about four hours. Just before serving, add spaghetti and cook until done.

Vivian Lydle, Drummond Island, MI

Aubergine Soup

1 lb. aubergine (eggplant), peeled and diced
6 Tbsp. oil, a combination of olive and other
4 tomatoes, peeled and chopped
2 onions, finely chopped
2 cloves garlic, minced

2 tsp. fresh basil, chopped
½ tsp. marjoram
1½ quarts chicken or meat stock
3 Tbsp. rice
Salt and freshly ground pepper
Parmesan cheese, grated

In a Dutch oven or other large kettle, fry the eggplant in the heated oil until pieces are nicely browned. Add the tomatoes, onions, garlic and herbs. Cook over moderate heat until mixture is soft. Add the stock and rice and cook until done. Season to taste with salt and pepper. Serve in bowls topped with Parmesan cheese.

Kathy Brandis, Camden, ME

STEWS

Poor Man's Stew

¼ lb. salt pork
1 quart water
Pepper
Celery seed
2 quarts green beans,
  sliced

1 quart potatoes,
  chopped
1 pint cream
Generous piece of butter

Remove and discard rind from salt pork, and dice. Put in a good sized pot, add water, some pepper, a sprinkle of celery seed; cook until tender. Add the green beans and cook until almost tender. Add the potatoes and cook until potatoes are done. Add the cream and butter, heat to boiling point, and serve in bowls with crackers.

Olive Edson, East Randolph, VT

Wilder Stew

About 1 lb. stew meat,
  cut into chunks
Salt and pepper
1 clove garlic, minced
Worcestershire sauce

Turnips, chopped
Potatoes, chopped
Carrots, chopped
Celery, chopped

Cook stew meat in water until it's soft. As it reaches the soft stage, add salt and pepper, garlic and Worcestershire. Cook the vegetables separately, each in its own pot, and save the juices. Layer everything in a two-pound coffee can, warm it up, and there's the stew. This way there's more control: all the vegetables retain their shape and texture.

Perry Wilder, Colrain, MA

September Stew

In the late summer, take a deep heavy pot or frying pan, put a little oil in the bottom, and sauté some onion and ground beef (one-half to one pound). Then put in layers of vegetables according to how long they need to cook—green beans, squash, tomatoes (green or red) and whatever else the garden grew too much of—putting the toughest on the bottom. Put on lid and let it all cook over low heat until vegetables are tender. There is no liquid added and few vitamins lost.

Audrey Lyle, Alstead, NH

Quick Garden Stew   Serves 4

Although I have listed specific vegetables to use, whatever is ripe will do.

1 can chicken broth
1 Tbsp. tamari sauce
2 tomatoes, chopped
1 onion, diced
1 cup green beans, chopped
½ cup peas

2 potatoes, diced
½ cup summer squash, diced
½ cup zucchini, diced
Fresh basil and parsley, chopped

In either a wok or Dutch oven, set directly over the flame, bring the chicken broth and tamari sauce to a boil. Add the tomatoes, onions, and toughest vegetables first. Cover pot and cook about eight minutes, or until almost tender. Add the remaining vegetables and herbs and cook until all is tender, but not soggy. Serve.

"A stew boiled is a stew spoiled."

The Century Cook Book, 1894

Texas Beef Stew

2 lbs. beef brisket
1 beef bone
2 quarts water
2½ tsp. salt
¼ tsp. pepper
1 leek, chopped
1 cup onion, chopped
1 cup green pepper,
  chopped

1 cup carrots, sliced
1 cup celery, diced
1 cup potatoes, diced
1 can tomatoes (16 oz.)
1½ tsp. chili powder
½ tsp. ground cumin
2 medium zucchini, sliced

Place meat, bone, water, salt and pepper in a heavy pot. Cover and bring to a boil. Skim off any foam that rises. Simmer for about two hours, or until meat is tender. Cool and chill in the refrigerator several hours, or overnight. Remove and scrape off hardened fat. Add leek, onion, green pepper, carrot, celery, potatoes, tomatoes, chili powder and cumin. Simmer over low heat for one hour. Remove from heat. Remove bone and meat from stock and trim off fat, cutting meat into bite-sized pieces. Place meat and zucchini in stock, bring to a boil, and simmer over low heat for half an hour.

Stan Black, Concord, MA

Gwen's Stew

Order a brisket from butcher. Sear both sides in a cast-iron Dutch oven. Add a little oil and barely brown two sliced onions. Add one can tomato purée, salt, pepper, three bay leaves, and one-half teaspoon ground cumin. Simmer at back of stove all day. Add one tablespoon vinegar. Serve with buckwheat groats or rice. Tastes best the following day.

Gwen Robinson, Orford, NH

Great Goulash

2 Tbsp. lard or oil
2 medium onions, finely chopped
2 cloves garlic, minced
3 Tbsp. sweet Hungarian paprika
2 lbs. stewing meat, cut into 1½-inch cubes
½ tsp. caraway seeds
4 cups chicken or beef stock
½ tsp. salt
4 peppercorns
2 medium-sized potatoes, cut into 1-inch cubes
1½ cups tomatoes, peeled and finely chopped
2 green peppers, finely chopped
1 lb. mushrooms, cleaned and halved
½ tsp. marjoram

In a Dutch oven or other heavy pot, heat the lard until a light haze forms over it. Move pot to a moderate heat and add the onions and garlic. Cook until onions are lightly browned, remove from heat, and stir in paprika. Add the meat, caraway seeds, stock, salt and peppercorns. Bring liquid to a boil, cover and set aside to simmer until the beef is almost tender. Add the potatoes, tomatoes, peppers, mushrooms, and marjoram. Simmer for another thirty to forty minutes or until the vegetables and meat are tender. Skim off any fat. Serve as is or with a dollop of sour cream.

Brunswick Stew

1 roasting hen, 5 to 6 lbs., disjointed
3 Tbsp. bacon drippings
1 medium onion, sliced
1½ cups tomatoes, peeled and quartered
2 packages frozen lima beans
1 cup chicken broth
3 whole cloves
Salt and pepper
3 cups corn, fresh or frozen
2 tsp. Worcestershire sauce
1 cup toasted bread crumbs

In a Dutch oven, brown the chicken in the bacon drippings. Remove the chicken and sauté the onion until golden brown. Return chicken to pot and add tomatoes, lima beans, chicken broth and cloves. Salt and pepper to taste. Cover and slowly simmer for a couple of hours, or until chicken is tender. Add the corn and continue to cook until meat is ready to fall from bones. Add Worcestershire sauce, stir in bread crumbs and serve immediately.

Cathy Cooper, Ann Arbor, MI

Rick's Stew   Serves 6

2 lbs. stew meat, cubed
Flour
3 Tbsp. bacon drippings
1 can tomato paste
1 clove garlic, minced
1½ cups rosé wine
2 whole cloves
1 bay leaf
3 large carrots, chopped
3 potatoes, diced
2 medium onions, sliced
2 tart apples, sliced
4 stalks celery, sliced

Shake meat with flour in a paper bag so that all sides are well coated. In a Dutch oven brown meat in bacon drippings. Add tomato paste, garlic, wine, cloves, and bay leaf. Bake in a medium oven for forty-five minutes. Remove and add carrots.

Cook one-half hour longer and add potatoes, onions and apples. Cook forty-five minutes and add celery. If liquid is too low, add more wine. Cook one-half hour longer.

Rick Yeiser, Concord, MA

Cajun Shrimp Stew   Serves 4-6

1 Tbsp. cooking fat
½ cup flour
1 large green pepper, chopped
1 cup celery, chopped
3 cloves garlic, minced
1 large onion, chopped
1 can tomato sauce or paste
1 cup water
2 lbs. fresh or frozen shrimp, shelled and deveined
2 lemon slices
½ tsp. salt
½ tsp. Worcestershire sauce

In a Dutch oven, heat the cooking fat and stir in flour. Add the green pepper, celery, garlic, and onion. Cook and stir until limp. Add tomato paste and water. Cover and simmer slowly for forty-five minutes. Add shrimp, lemon, salt, and Worcestershire sauce. Cook about twenty minutes longer.

Wendy Wolf, New Orleans, LA

MAIN DISHES: TOP-OF-THE-STOVE, WOK, AND BAKED

CHICKEN

Fried Chicken

A Martha's Vineyard recipe.

Dip pieces in beaten egg and then crushed, seasoned saltines. Refrigerate an hour or more, dip again in crumbs and fry.

Gwen Robinson, Orford, NH

Chicken and Walnuts   Serves 4

1 lb. chicken breasts,
  cut into ½-inch cubes
¼ cup soy sauce
2 Tbsp. cornstarch
6 Tbsp. peanut oil
1 cup blanched walnuts

2 or 3 slices ginger root,
  or 1 tsp. powder, or
  candied
1 Tbsp. saki or sherry
1 tsp. sugar

Mix the chicken with soy sauce and one tablespoon cornstarch. Heat wok or heavy skillet, put in oil and add walnuts. Fry to a light brown and remove immediately, as walnuts easily burn. Place chicken and ginger in hot oil and stir until chicken changes color. Stir in remaining cornstarch mixed with wine and sugar. Add walnuts. Stir until liquid clears, and serve. This is excellent spooned over rice.

Oriental Chicken with   Serves 4
Cashews

2 eggs
¼ cup unsifted flour
1 Tbsp. sugar
½ tsp. salt
1 Tbsp. water
2 tsp. dry sherry

2 whole chicken breasts
  (3/4 pound), boned and
  skinned
1 cup salted cashews,
  finely chopped (I do it in
  a blender)
1 cup peanut oil

Beat the eggs slightly. Add flour, sugar, salt, water, and sherry. Beat until smooth. Thinly slice chicken parallel to the grain into pieces about 2 inches long. Dip chicken pieces in egg mixture and then coat them with chopped cashews. Heat peanut oil in wok. Cook chicken, a few pieces at a time, two to three minutes until done. Drain on paper towels. Keep warm until ready to serve. Warming ovens are handy for this.

Cook Stove Cream Chicken   Serves 4

Butter or margarine for
  browning
1 large chicken, cut into parts
Flour to dredge

Salt and pepper
5 or 6 whole allspice
½ cup water
2 cups heavy cream

Melt butter or margarine in a Dutch oven. Dredge chicken parts in flour and brown. Add the salt and pepper to taste, and add allspice. Pour in water; it should be enough to cover the bottom of the pan and loosen the brown bits. After it has simmered this way for about thirty minutes, add the cream and continue simmering slowly until tender. (If browned on direct flame burner, replace cover on burner and let fire sufficiently die to simmer chicken slowly for three to four hours, depending on size of chicken.) Serve with mashed potatoes or riced potatoes as the cream gravy is delicious.

Helen Kilgore, CA

Lime-Fried Chicken   Serves 3-4

1 small chicken, cut into
  pieces
3 or 4 fresh limes, squeezed
Oil or fat for frying

1 onion, sliced in thin rings
Flour for dredging
Salt, pepper, paprika

Rub each chicken piece with lime juice. Marinate at least one hour at room temperature or two hours or more in the refrigerator. Heat the oil for frying in a large heavy skillet and add the onion rings. Shake the chicken pieces in the seasoned flour and add them to the skillet. Brown on all sides over high heat, then move to a slower lid and cook for one-half hour, turning now and then. Drain well on paper towels and serve along with onions, which stick to the chicken and make it crunch.

Chicken with Almonds   Serves 4

3 Tbsp. raisins	1 tsp. salt
3 Tbsp. rum	¼ tsp. pepper
¼ cup slivered almonds	3/4 cup chicken broth
¼ cup butter	3 tsp. cornstarch
2 whole chicken breasts, skinned and boned	½ cup heavy cream

Soak raisins in rum. In a large skillet, brown almonds in melted butter; remove. Add chicken breasts, salt and pepper. Cook ten minutes, turning often. Remove from skillet. Add the chicken broth and bring to a boil. Mix cornstarch and cream and add to the broth; stir constantly for three minutes. Stir in rum and raisins and reheat chicken breasts gently in sauce. Serve topped with almonds.

C. Hillnian, NY

Perfect Poultry Pie   Serves 4

Sauté onions, green pepper, mushrooms, carrots, and celery until almost tender. Add cooked chicken, one can cream of mushroom soup, dry white wine, sour cream, and a little milk. Pour it all into a pie crust that you have baked slightly or brushed with egg white. Cover with top crust, slit, and bake at 350°F. till done.

Sherry Goetting, Madison, CT

SEAFOOD

Fricasseed Oysters

One quart of large fresh oysters; half a pint of water; one tablespoonful of green parsley washed and cut up fine; one teaspoonful of crushed celery seed; one gill (½ cup) of rich sweet milk; two teaspoonsful of flour; three yolks of fresh eggs; three ounces of fresh butter; one teaspoonful of salt; half a teaspoonful of pepper; three tablespoonsful of crushed double baked rusk. Put the oysters into a colander and let cold water run through them. Put the half pint of water, parsley and celery seed into a saucepan and let it come to a boil, then put in the milk. Mix the flour with a spoonful of cold milk, then beat the yolks and flour together and stir them in. Stir it until the yolks thicken, but it must not boil. Then put in the butter, salt, pepper, and the oysters. As soon as the oysters are fringed and swollen, (they must not boil) stir in the rusk, take them quickly off the fire and put them into a warm chafing-dish.

Domestic Cookery, 1888

Fried Fish

Get a hot and fast fire going with cedar slab or popple wood. Put the frying pan over the hottest griddle and put in Crisco, or other non-saturated fat, to a depth of a quarter-inch. Wait until it smokes. Dip fish in flour seasoned with salt and pepper, and fast-fry them in the pan. Keep adding wood to keep the fire hot. I never would use any other kind of stove for frying fish; this is the best.

Mary Garchow, Drummond Island, MI

The Shrimp of Hearts   Serves 8

2½ cups mushrooms, sliced
  ¼ cup butter
  5 Tbsp. flour
  ½ cup milk
  2 cups light cream
  ½ tsp. salt
  ½ tsp. Worcestershire sauce
  Few drops of Tabasco

2 Tbsp. fresh parsley,
  chopped
2 Tbsp. onion, minced
2 1 lb. cans artichoke
  hearts, drained
2 lb. medium-sized
  shrimp, peeled and de-
  veined
½ cup Gruyère cheese

Sauté mushrooms in butter for five minutes and add flour. Stir for about three minutes. Gradually stir in milk and cream; add salt, Worcestershire, Tabasco, parsley and onion. Cook over moderate heat, stirring constantly, until thickened. Remove from heat. In a greased, shallow casserole, arrange the artichoke hearts; place shrimp over hearts. Pour in the mushroom sauce and sprinkle with cheese. Bake, uncovered, in a moderate oven for about twenty to thirty minutes, or until heated through.

Burmese Shrimp   Serves 4

4 Tbsp. oil
2 cups onions, finely sliced
2 lbs. raw shrimp, shelled
  and de-veined
4 Tbsp. saki or dry white
  wine

2½ tsp. soy sauce
3/4 tsp. chili powder
  1 Tbsp. ginger
  ½ tsp. saffron
  2 cups sour cream

In a wok or heavy skillet, heat oil and sauté onions until limp. Remove. Add the shrimp and fry until both sides are browned. Add the wine, soy sauce, chili powder, ginger, and saffron. Cook covered for about ten minutes over medium heat. Stir in sour cream and onions and cook until hot, but do not boil. Serve with rice.

Baked Fish

Oil, any kind, but do add
    at least some olive oil
Lemon juice
Onion juice
Fresh or dry herbs:

oregano, basil,
marjoram, bay leaves,
tarragon
Minced garlic
2-3 lbs. fish

Make a marinade of the oil, lemon and onion juice, herbs and garlic. The amount of each is determined by taste. Scale, clean, and wash the fish. Make a few incisions in the skin and soak in the marinade for a few hours. Wrap the fish in a piece of well-oiled foil and bake in a moderate oven for about one hour. The flesh will flake easily with a fork and will have lost its translucence when done.

Minced Clam and Eggplant Casserole   Serves 3-4

1 medium eggplant
Oil
1 10½ oz. can minced clams
1 Tbsp. onion, minced
2 Tbsp. butter

1 cup bread crumbs,
    seasoned with salt,
    pepper, sage, marjoram,
    basil
1 can mushroom soup

Slice, peel, and dice eggplant. Heat oil in a heavy skillet until quite hot and brown eggplant. Cover the bottom of a greased casserole with half of it. Sauté onion in butter until golden; mix in bread crumbs. Add half of this to casserole. Spread drained clams on top, and layer with eggplant, then bread crumbs. Pour mushroom soup, thinned with clam juice, on top. Bake in a moderate oven for thirty minutes, or until brown.

Lindsay Olson, Flint, MI

Clam Fritters

2 eggs, beaten
10 to 12 saltines, rolled
    into crumbs
1 small onion, finely
    chopped
Salt and pepper
1 clove garlic, minced

½ tsp. dill
1 tsp. Worcestershire
    sauce
2 drops Tabasco
1 pint clams, minced or
    ground
3 Tbsp. oil

Combine everything, except oil, and mix well. Heat the oil in a heavy pan or wok and drop clam mixture by tablespoonfuls. Cook on each side about five minutes, or until crispy. If fritters burn, move pan to a lower heat. Add oil as needed.

Suzanne Terry, Irvington, VA

Wine Steamed Fish

Dry white wine
1 Tbsp. soy sauce
1 small piece ginger root,
    finely chopped

2 scallions, finely chopped
Fish fillets, haddock, sole,
    flounder, cod
Cornstarch

Place either a vegetable steamer or chopsticks (laid crosshatched to form a platform) in the bottom of a wok. Add wine to about one-half inch beneath the platform and add soy sauce, ginger root and scallions. Bring wine to a boil and lay fish fillets on platform. Cover wok and steam until fish flesh is white. Remove fish to a platter and add enough cornstarch to wine to form a medium-thick sauce. Pour over fish and serve.

MEAT

Beirut Kibbeh   Serves 8

1 cup bulgar
4 cups hot water
2 lbs. lean beef or lamb,
    ground
1 tsp. salt
½ tsp. cinnamon
¼ tsp. allspice
Dash of cloves
Dash of freshly ground
    pepper

½ cup onion, chopped
1/3 cup walnuts, finely
    chopped
¼ tsp. salt
½ tsp. cinnamon
¼ tsp. allspice
Dash of cloves
Dash of pepper
1 recipe Tangy Yogurt
    Sauce

In a mixing bowl, combine the bulgur and hot water. Let stand about 15 minutes, or until puffed up. In a separate bowl, combine 1½ lbs. of meat, 1 tsp. salt, ½ tsp. cinnamon, ¼ tsp. allspice, first dash of cloves, and first dash of pepper. Mix well. Drain the bulgur, kneading or squeezing until moisture is gone. Combine bulgur and meat mixture and mix thoroughly. In a skillet, cook the remaining meat and onion until meat is browned and onion is tender. Add the walnuts and remaining spices, and remove from heat. Pat half the bulgur/meat mixture into the bottom of a 9 x 9 x 2 baking pan. Cover with the browned meat mixture. Top with the remaining bulgur/meat. Bake in a moderate oven for forty to forty-five minutes. Serve with Tangy Yogurt Sauce (p. 116), and you have a wonderful meal.

South African Bobotie   Serves 8

3 Tbsp. butter	2 tsp. salt
1½ cups onion, chopped	2 Tbsp. plum jam
2 cups fresh bread crumbs	2 Tbsp. lemon juice
½ cup milk	¼ cup blanched almonds,
3 lbs. chuck beef or lamb,	ground
ground	3 bay leaves
1 egg, beaten	2 lemons, thinly sliced
2 Tbsp. curry powder	2 pimiento strips

In a small skillet, melt the butter and sauté onion until golden. In a mixing bowl, soak bread crumbs in milk. Add the meat, egg, onion, curry, salt, jam, lemon juice and almonds; mix thoroughly. On the bottom of an ungreased ten-inch pie plate or round baking dish, place the bay leaves; on top, pat in the meat mixture. Bake in a 350°F. oven for an hour. Drain off any moisture. Serve with lemon slices arranged around the border. In the center, lay a lemon slice that has been cut halfway through and twisted with a thin pimiento strip on either side. Serve in wedges.

Keeping Meat in Snow: An excellent way to keep fresh meat during the winter is practiced by the farmers in the country which they term "salting in snow." Take a large clean tub, cover the bottom three or four inches thick with clean snow; then lay in pieces of fresh meat, spare-ribs, fowls or whatever you wish to keep, and cover each layer with two or three inches of snow, taking particular care to fill snow into every crevice between the pieces, and around the edges of the tub. Fowls must be filled inside with the snow. The last layer in the tub must be snow, pressed down tight; then cover the tub and keep in a cool place—the colder the better. The meat will not freeze; and, unless the weather should be very warm, the snow will not thaw, but the meat will remain as fresh and juicy as when it was killed.

Mrs. Hale's New Cookbook, 1873

Tangy Yogurt Sauce

3 chicken bouillon cubes
3 tsp. cornstarch
1 cup water

3 Tbsp. lemon juice
1 egg, well beaten
1 cup plain yogurt

In a saucepan, combine bouillon and cornstarch. Stir in water and lemon juice. Cook and stir until thickened and bubbly. In a small mixing bowl, stir together the egg and yogurt. Stir about one-half cup of the hot mixture into the egg mixture. Return contents to saucepan, cooking and stirring over low heat for two minutes more.

Beef Yat Sen   Serves 6

1 lb. flank steak, sliced
   paper thin
2 Tbsp. cornstarch
2 Tbsp. soy sauce
4 Tbsp. peanut oil
1 medium onion, cut in
   1/8-inch slices

1 cup celery, sliced thin
6 large mushrooms
2 carrots, sliced thin
Salt
1 cup beef stock
Rice for 6 servings

Add meat to a mixture of cornstarch and soy sauce. In a heated wok or skillet, add two tablespoons oil; sauté onion for one minute. Add celery and cook two more minutes. Add mushrooms and carrots; cook one minute. Salt to taste and remove to a dish. Add remaining oil and drop in meat slices. Cook and stir until meat just loses pinkness. Add vegetables, toss together, and add stock. As soon as it comes to a boil, remove from heat and serve immediately over rice.

Laura Sheppard, Williamstown, MA

My Favorite Liver   Serves 3-4

Usually I can't even swallow liver, but prepared this way, I do it happily.

½ cup dry white wine
2 Tbsp. soy sauce
1 lb. liver, sliced into
   matchsticks

3 Tbsp. peanut oil
3 tart apples, sliced
2 medium onions, thinly
   sliced

Combine wine and soy sauce; marinate liver in this mixture for at least two hours. Heat half the oil in a wok or skillet and fry apples and onions until just limp. Remove. Add the remaining oil and fry liver until pinkness is gone. Add the apples and onions, cook and stir until it is well heated. Serve with rice or cooked bulgur.

Italian Sausage Spaghetti Sauce

1 lb. hot Italian sausage
2 28 oz. cans tomatoes
1 12 oz. can tomato purée
3 onions, chopped
2 tsp. salt
1 tsp. sweet basil
½ tsp. sage

⅛ tsp. rosemary
2 bay leaves
3 or 4 cloves garlic,
   minced
1½ tsp. oregano
¼ tsp. tarragon
¼ tsp. thyme

Remove casing from sausage. Fry and drain fat. Mix tomatoes and purée with fried sausage in a large, heavy, enamel pot. Add the rest of the ingredients and mix. Cover pot, bring to a boil, then move pan over so that sauce just bubbles. Simmer for three hours. Remove from heat and let stand covered overnight. Reheat just before serving.

Paul Falcone, East Randolph, VT

Tacos Gringo   Serves 8

2 Tbsp. oil
2 large onions, finely
   chopped
1-2 cloves garlic, minced
3 lbs. ground beef or pork
2 cans kidney beans
2 tomatoes, peeled and
   chopped
1 tsp. salt

2-3 tsp. chili powder
1-2 tsp. cumin
3 tsp. Worcestershire
   sauce
Generous dash of
   Tabasco
1 can tortillas (or see
   recipe, page 159)

In a heavy pot or Dutch oven, heat the oil and sauté onions
and garlic. Add meat and brown. Add beans, tomatoes, and
seasonings; cook over medium-low heat for about two hours,
stirring every so often. Fold tortillas in half and either warm
in the oven or fry until crispy in oil. Spoon meat mixture into
pocket and top with the following accompaniments:

chopped tomatoes
diced onions
grated cheese

chopped green peppers
shredded lettuce
sour cream

Seven Layer Casserole

1 layer potatoes
1 layer green peppers
1 layer onions
1 layer dry rice (¾ cup)

1 layer peas
1 lb. hamburg
1 can tomatoes
3 slices bacon

Salt, pepper and butter each layer. Pour can of tomatoes over
all and lay strips of bacon on top. Bake in casserole about two
hours. This is much much better baked in a wood stove oven.

Carolyn T. Kelley, Camden, ME

New England Boiled Dinner

"This recipe has been used in our family for over 100 years. There was always enough left over the next day to make Red Flannel Hash, the grand finale to a boiled dinner."

Olive Edson, East Randolph, VT

Big chunk of partially
  cooked corned beef
½ lb. salt pork
1 turnip, sliced
12 medium beets, washed
  with one inch of the tops
  left on

12 medium carrots, washed
12 medium onions
Potatotes
Few stalks of celery,
  with leaves, chopped

Put the corned beef into a large kettle filled one-third full of boiling water. Add the salt pork (this provides the salt for the whole business; back in those days, salt was an item of luxury). Add the turnips, beets (by leaving on the skins and part of the tops, the beets won't "bleed"), carrots, and onions. Simmer until vegetables are nearly done, and add as many whole potatoes as the kettle holds, and still have enough water to cook. Add the chopped celery. Simmer until potatoes are cooked. Put the meat in the center of a large platter and place the vegetables around so that they're colorfully arranged. Rub butter over the vegetables and serve with pickles, relishes, and homemade biscuits.

Red Flannel Hash

Grind everything that's leftover from the Boiled Dinner and put in a large iron spider with a generous amount of cream and butter. Season to taste. Heat until bubbling hot. To make it crusty, add more butter and cook longer, but turn frequently to keep it from burning.

Olive Edson, East Randolph, VT

VEGETARIAN

Mushroom-Bulgur Casserole

1½ cups cream of mushroom
    soup
1½ cups bulgur
2 Tbsp. butter
3 cups mushrooms, sliced
1 medium onion, chopped
1 clove garlic, minced

1 cup sour cream
3 Tbsp. dry sherry
½ cup sunflower seeds
½ cup cashews
    Salt and pepper to taste
    Sesame seeds
    Wheat germ

Bring soup to a boil and add bulgur; mix and set aside. In a
Dutch oven, melt butter and gently sauté mushrooms,
onion, and garlic until limp. Add sour cream and sherry; cook
three minutes. To bulgur mixture, add sunflower seeds,
cashews, salt and pepper; mix well. Stir into mushroom/
sour cream mixture. Garnish with sesame seeds and wheat
germ. Bake in a moderate oven for twenty minutes.

David Shepler, East Randolph, VT

Pasta e Faciola

6 cups water
½ lb. elbow macaroni
2 cups chick peas, or
    kidney beans, or
    combination of both,
    cooked

2 Tbsp. olive oil
1 onion, chopped
1 cup tomato sauce

Bring water to a boil and add macaroni and beans. While that
is cooking, heat olive oil and sauté onion and tomato
sauce. When macaroni finishes cooking (should be *al dente)*,
add tomato sauce to the water. Mix and serve in bowls.

Carolyn Tonnelli-Knight, Bethel, VT

Fava Salad

Served with Romaine lettuce leaves and Arab bread, this is a great lunch.

7 Tbsp. olive oil
2 onions, finely chopped
2½ cups water
1 cup dried fava beans, soaked 24 hours
Juice of 1 lemon
Salt
1 Tbsp. fresh dill, finely chopped

¼ tsp. paprika
¼ tsp. cayenne
2½ Tbsp. olive oil
Juice of ½ lemon
3 Tbsp. parsley, finely chopped

In a heavy pot, heat olive oil and sauté onions until transparent. Add 2½ cups water and bring to a boil. Drain beans and add to the pot; cook over low heat until beans collapse, about 1½ hours. Add more cooking water if necessary, but most should be absorbed by the time beans are done. In a blender or a bowl, mash beans to a paste. Add lemon juice, salt, dill, paprika, and cayenne. Pour this into a serving bowl and chill. Before serving, top with olive oil, lemon juice, and parsley.

Carolyn Cooper, Tucson, AZ

Three teaspoons of fresh herbs are equal to one teaspoon of dried.

Mediterranean Crunch

3 cups chicken broth, or
  1 cup water, 2 cups
  tomato juice
1-2 cloves garlic, minced
½ tsp. cumin
¼ tsp. tumeric
⅛ tsp. cayenne

1½ cups brown rice
2 Tbsp. oil
¾ cup walnuts, chopped
1 medium onion, chopped
1½ cups chick peas, cooked
Handful of fresh parsley,
  chopped

Combine liquid, garlic, cumin, tumeric, and cayenne in a pot, bring to a boil, and add rice. Cover, move to where it simmers, and cook until done. Add more liquid if necessary. In a large skillet or wok, heat oil and fry walnuts until brown; remove immediately. Sauté onions until transparent and add rice and chick peas. Fry until thoroughly heated; toss in walnuts. Transfer to a serving bowl and garnish with parsley.

Spicy Rice   Serves 2

3 cups vegetable or chicken
  broth
1 cup brown rice
1 clove garlic, minced
2 Tbsp. oil
1 medium onion, chopped

½ green pepper, chopped
2 stalks celery, chopped
½ cup raisins
1 Tbsp. soy sauce
2 tsp. vinegar
2 tsp. molasses

Bring broth to a boil and add rice and garlic. Cover pot, move to simmer, and cook until done. To a large skillet or wok, add oil and fry onion, green pepper, and celery until crisply tender. Add raisins; cook about one minute more. Add rice; cook and stir until thoroughly heated. Mix together soy sauce, vinegar, and molasses; pour over rice mixture. Toss and serve.

Eggplant-Apple Curry   Serves 4

2 Tbsp. oil
1 eggplant, cut into
   one-inch chunks
2 onions, chopped
3 apples, chopped

½ cup raisins
2 tsp. curry powder
Apple cider, optional
Salt and pepper

Heat oil in a large skillet and sauté the eggplant, onion, and apple. When approaching tenderness, add the raisins, curry powder, cider, and seasonings. Cook and stir until tender. Serve with rice.

Barbara Ernst, East Randolph, VT

Marinara Sauce for Spaghetti

A simple, quick, and delicious spaghetti sauce.

6 cloves garlic
¼ cup olive oil

1 quart canned tomatoes
2 handfuls parsley, chopped

In a skillet set over low heat, soften the garlic in the olive oil. Do not brown. Add the tomatoes and parsley and cook fifteen minutes over medium heat.

Carolyn Tonnelli-Knight, Bethel, VT

Many kinds of beans require long cooking hours to soften, something for which the wood range is well-suited. Don't add salt to the cooking water as that inhibits the softening. Set the pot of water and beans over moderate heat and be patient; but for faster results, first soak the beans overnight, or use a pressure cooker.

Saucy Soybean Curry   Serves 2-3

2 Tbsp. oil
1 medium onion, chopped
1 large tart apple, finely
  chopped
4 stalks celery, sliced
1½ cups chicken broth or
  tomato juice

2 Tbsp. flour
2 tsp. curry powder
½ tsp. cumin
1 tsp. salt
½ tsp. paprika
1 cup raisins
3 cups soybeans, cooked

In a heavy skillet, heat oil and sauté onion, apples, and celery. Add the broth or tomato juice. Make a paste of the flour, curry powder, cumin, salt and paprika with a little water. Stir paste into vegetables. Add raisins and soybeans; cover and let simmer for fifteen minutes.

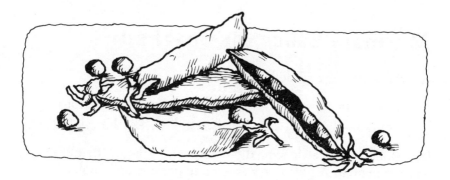

CHEESE AND EGGS

Quiche

Add enough water to 1½ cups flour to make sticky, wet dough. Roll out small pieces paper thin, using all the flour you need, into any shape. Fry a few seconds on each side in greased skillet until barely set. Overlap pieces in large pie plate, letting them hang over rim. The more uneven the edges, the more pleasing the result.

For a filling, use crumbled fried bacon, chopped, sautéed onion, mixed grated cheeses, and anything else to your fancy. Pour in seven well-beaten eggs and about two cups mixed cream and milk, and sprinkle with paprika. Bake on rack until risen and well-browned in hot oven. Delicious cold. For vegetarians, line crust with re-fried beans instead of bacon.

Gwen Robinson, Orford, NH

For all quiche fillings: prepare a crust and either bake in a hot oven for ten minutes, or brush an unbaked crust with egg white—either way prevents it from becoming soggy. The crust must be cool before filling it. To test quiche for doneness, insert a knife into the custard one inch from the pastry edge. If it comes out clean, the quiche is done. Let the quiche rest ten minutes before serving.

Sherry's Baked Stuffed Manicotti

1 eggplant
2 cups cottage cheese
1 clove garlic, minced
1 onion, chopped and
   sautéed
1 egg

½ tsp. oregano
Salt and pepper
Manicotti
Tomato sauce
Parmesan cheese, grated

Bake eggplant one hour in a moderate oven. Remove pulp and mash. Mix it with cottage cheese, garlic, onion, egg, oregano, salt, and pepper. Parboil manicotti. Stuff it with eggplant mixture; place in a baking dish. Cover with tomato sauce and top with a generous amount of grated cheese. Bake covered for twenty minutes. Uncover and add more cheese and bake ten minutes more.

Sherry Streeter, Madison, CT

Pizza

Dough:

2 cups lukewarm water	2 tsp. salt
2 Tbsp. dry yeast	3 Tbsp. oil
2 tsp. honey	6 cups wholewheat flour

Topping:

Tomato sauce	Mozzarella, cheddar, and
Sliced tomatoes	Parmesan cheese, grated
Peppers	Olive oil
Onions	Salt, pepper, oregano
Sausage	

For dough: mix together water and yeast and let stand five minutes. Stir in honey, salt, and oil. Add three cups of flour and beat until smooth. Add last three cups of flour and knead until barely firm. Let stand ten minutes. Divide in half. Roll out to fit a greased cookie sheet or divide into four and grease four pie pans. Let rise about ten minutes. Cover each with topping ingredients. Bake in a moderate oven (375°F.) for twenty-five minutes.

Barbara McCarthy, Wileyville, WV

Extra pizza dough can be frozen for later use. A deep dish pizza can be made by stretching dough to cover the bottom and one and one-half inches of the sides of a large, cast-iron skillet.

Spanakopita

2 lbs. spinach, washed, stemmed, and shredded
1 cup spring onions, chopped
1/3 cup olive oil
4 oz. feta cheese, crumbled
1 cup cottage cheese
3 Tbsp. Parmesan cheese, grated
2 Tbsp. parsley, chopped
1 tsp. fresh dill or fennel, chopped
4 eggs, lightly beaten
¼ tsp. nutmeg
Salt and pepper
8 oz. filo pastry
Olive oil for assembling pie

Place spinach in a vegetable steamer or colander over boiling water and steam for eight minutes. Drain off all moisture and place in a bowl to cool. Gently fry onions in oil until soft; add onions to spinach. Stir in cheeses, herbs, eggs, nutmeg, and season to taste with salt and pepper. Lightly oil an oven dish (14" x 10"). Line dish with five sheets of filo pastry, brushing each sheet with oil. Add spinach filling and spread evenly. Moisten edges of top layer of filo with water and place remainder of filo on top. Brush with oil and bake in a moderately hot oven (375°F.) for forty-five minutes. Remove from oven and let stand five minutes before cutting into squares.

Ann Spear, Salt Lake City, UT

Eggplant Casserole Italiano

I never use exact proportions when I cook, but this recipe is good, no matter how much you use of what. If you don't have all the vegetables called for, just use what's in the refrigerator or garden. But be sure to use fresh parsley—that's the secret of good Italian cooking.

Carolyn Tonnelli-Knight, Bethel, VT

Very fresh eggplant, cubed with skin
Potatoes, sliced thin with skins
Fresh or canned tomatoes
Onions, finely chopped
Green pepper, finely chopped
Mushrooms, sliced
Grated cheese
Wheat germ
Fresh parsley, chopped
1-2 eggs (depending on quantity), well-beaten

Steam the eggplant and potatoes for fifteen minutes, until partially soft. Over a medium heat, sauté the tomatoes, onion, green pepper, and mushrooms to make a sauce. Mix together the cheese, wheat germ, parsley and eggs. In a baking dish, layer with eggplant/potato, then cheese mixture, then sauce. Repeat. Bake in a moderate oven until custard has set.

Cauliflower Quiche   Serves 4

2 cups cauliflowerets, ½-inch thick
1 9" pie shell
½ cup slivered almonds, toasted
2 eggs
½ cup milk
½ cup mayonnaise
2 cups cheddar cheese, grated
Pinch of nutmeg
Sprinkle of freshly ground pepper

Steam cauliflowerets over boiling water until just crisply tender (about ten minutes). Plunge into cold water to cool quickly; drain. Place cauliflowerets on bottom of pie shell and sprinkle with almonds. In an electric blender or mixer or with a briskly moving arm, combine eggs, milk, mayonnaise, 1¼ cups cheese, pepper, and nutmeg; blend until smooth. Pour over cauliflower and nuts. Sprinkle with remaining cheese. Bake in a moderate-hot (375°F.) oven.

Roquefort Quiche   Serves 4

¼ lb. bacon
4 oz. Roquefort cheese
2 cups sour cream
2 Tbsp. butter
1 small onion, minced
5-6 large mushrooms,
  chopped
¼ tsp. garlic salt

Pinch of mace
Sprinkle of freshly
  ground pepper
3 eggs, well beaten
2 Tbsp. dry white wine
1 Tbsp. cornstarch
1 9" pie shell

Fry bacon until crisp; crumble and set aside. Mash the cheese and mix with sour cream. In a heavy saucepan, melt butter and sauté onion and mushrooms until limp. Stir in Roquefort mixture, garlic salt, mace, and pepper. Beat eggs with wine and cornstarch; stir into Roquefort mixture. Pour into pie shell. Bake in a moderate-hot (375°F.) oven.

Baked Spinach Omelet   Serves 2 generously

4 eggs, separated
1 package spinach, cooked
  and drained
4 Tbsp. milk
1 tsp. salt

½ tsp. freshly ground
  pepper
Pinch of nutmeg
1 Tbsp. butter
¼ cup Parmesan cheese

Beat egg whites until stiff. Beat yolks slightly; blend with cooked spinach and milk. Add salt, pepper, and nutmeg. Fold in egg whites. In a medium-sized skillet, melt the butter. Pour in egg mixture and cook over low heat until the bottom sets and lightly browns. Sprinkle cheese over top and bake in a moderate oven until omelet is firm and cheese browns.

A Fabulous Fondue

One of the most entertaining parties I've ever attended was given by a friend who had cooked a big pot of fondue on his wood stove. He set an enormous basket of homemade French bread chunks to one side and all the guests formed a circle and walked around the stove, dipping into the pot as they passed. This is his recipe—and you don't have to walk around the stove to enjoy it.

1 clove garlic

For each person:	1 tsp. flour
	¾ glass dry white wine,
2 parts Gruyere cheese,	Chablis or Neufchatelle
grated	Pinches of pepper and
1 part medium or sharp	sweet basil
cheddar cheese, grated	Kirsch

Use a Dutch oven or heavy casserole dish. Rub the insides with a clove of garlic. Add the grated cheese, flour, and about 4/5 of the wine. Over *low* heat, slowly melt the cheese: if it heats too fast, the oil will separate from the cheese and ruin the fondue. Stir cheese until it comes to a boil; add pepper, sweet basil, and kirsch to taste. (I like a lot of kirsch.) The texture should be thick but not stringy. If too thick, add the rest of the wine. To serve, keep casserole warm so that cheese is slowly bubbling—the far end of the wood stove is ideal. Dip in chunks of French bread or large pieces of cooked vegetables. Broccoli is particularly good.

David Shepler, East Randolph, VT

Egg dishes of any kind should not be cooked over high heat or the texture becomes tough and rubbery.

Rigatoni Democrazia   Serves 8

The best pasta I've ever eaten!

1 lb. rigatoni
1 lb. hot Italian
  sausage, decased
1 lb. sweet Italian
  sausage, decased

1 clove garlic, minced
1 cup Parmesan or
  Romano cheese, grated
1½ sticks butter
1 pint heavy cream

Cook rigatoni following instructions on package. While it's cooking, sauté the sausage with garlic until browned and crispy. Drain rigatoni and place in a large pot. Add the sausage, cheese, butter and cream. Stir over moderate heat and serve.

Egg Foo Yung   Serves 6

7 eggs, beaten
3 cups Chinese cabbage,
  chopped
1 cup scallions, chopped
1 16 oz. can meatless chow
  mein, drained, saving
  the sauce

½ cup bamboo shoots
½ cup water chestnuts,
  sliced
1 Tbsp. soy sauce
½ lb. snow peas
Oil

Combine all the ingredients except oil. Get two small frying pans—about five-inch—smoking hot. Add one tablespoon oil and let heat until smoking again. Add ½-2/3 cup of the mixture and brown on the bottom. Flip over into the other pan, which is also heated and oiled. Cook about two more minutes, or until browned. As the frying pans are emptied, fill with more oil and more batter until all is cooked. Heat the drained sauce and pour over pancakes.

Paul Falcone, East Randolph, VT

BROILING AND ROASTING

BROILING

For broiling meats and fish, brush them with oil—particularly olive oil; this helps seal in the juices and enhances the flavor. Avoid excessively thick cuts of meat—1½-inches is about maximum—and trim off any hunks of fat. Grease the grill and lay on the meat. If using a stationary rather than camp-fire style grill, use tongs, rather than a fork, to turn the meat; it prevents piercing the flesh and losing the juices.

Chickens should be split in half, greased, and set on the grill cavity-side down; the bones will transfer enough heat to cook the flesh. Finish by browning the other side.

Broiled Cube Steaks

Place wire cake rack or chicken wire over top opening of wood burning section of stove. When wood is blazing like mad, take any old one-half-inch thick slice of chuck and beat it with the edge of a saucer till you've broken its spirit. Then salt, pepper, garlic, and Worcestershire sauce it. Throw it on the wire and turn it once when it's as rare or well done as you like it. The fat will splatter all over the wood and make a flame that looks like an inferno—but that's what makes it great!

Barbara Streeter, Madison, CT

Barbecued Spareribs   Serves 3-4

1 onion, finely chopped
2 cloves garlic, finely minced
2 cups tomato sauce
½ cup vinegar
½ cup molasses
½ tsp. ginger
¼ tsp. cloves

½ cup soy sauce
Freshly ground pepper
1 Tbsp. Worcestershire sauce
Tabasco to taste
8-10 meaty ribs, trimmed of fat

In a saucepan, combine all ingredients, except ribs, and simmer for about one-half hour. Pour over spare-ribs and marinate at least three hours at room temperature, longer in the refrigerator. Baste with sauce while broiling.

"Resist the greenhorn's temptation to cook hot dogs right on the surface. It's a mess!"

Gwen Robinson, Orford, NH

Bul Kogi

2 lbs. steak
3 Tbsp. soy sauce
2 Tbsp. oil, preferably
   sesame
2 Tbsp. brown sugar
1 thin slice ginger root,
   minced

2 green onions, finely
   chopped
1-2 cloves garlic, minced
2 Tbsp. sesame seeds
1 Tbsp. sherry
1 bouillon cube, mashed
Freshly ground pepper

Marinate steak(s) in a mixture of the remaining ingredients for at least three hours, but the longer, the tastier. Broil over coals.

Sesame Broiled Fish

1 lb. fish fillets
2 Tbsp. butter, melted
2 Tbsp. lemon juice
¼ tsp. paprika
¼ tsp. garlic salt

¼ tsp. freshly ground
   pepper
2 Tbsp. sesame seeds,
   toasted

Arrange fish on grill. Combine butter and lemon juice and brush over fillets. Sprinkle on paprika, garlic salt, pepper, and sesame seeds. Broil close to the coals. Fish is cooked when flesh flakes easily with a fork.

Honeyed Chicken

1/3 cup butter
1/3 cup honey
¼ cup Dijon mustard

2 tsp. Madras curry
1 frying chicken, cut into
   pieces

In a small saucepan, melt butter and add honey, mustard, and curry powder; brush over chicken. Broil slowly over coals, basting often.

Shish Kabob

2 lbs. lean beef, cut into
   1½-inch cubes
1 cup dry red wine
½ cup soy sauce
3 Tbsp. Worcestershire
   sauce
1 clove garlic, crushed

2 Tbsp. olive oil
1 large green pepper,
   chopped
12 whole mushrooms,
   cleaned
12 small onions
Freshly ground pepper

Combine all ingredients in a bowl and let stand at least eight hours in the refrigerator. Alternate meat, mushrooms, green pepper, and onions on skewers. Broil over hot coals, basting often with sauce.

T.J. Goetting, Odessa, MD

Souvlaki (Greek Skewered Meat)

1½ lbs. round steak, cut
   into 1½-inch cubes
½ cup olive oil
3 Tbsp. vinegar
⅛ tsp. pepper

¼ tsp. oregano
2 Tbsp. each of finely
   chopped carrots, celery,
   and onion

Marinate meat in remaining ingredients for three to four hours. Run skewers through meat cubes and set over top of the stove. Broil until tender and browned.

Philip Angell, Randolph Center, VT

"Broiling is best when the coals are glowing and just beginning to gray on top. The meat must be at room temperature. A sure way to remember this is to marinate it for two hours in wine. Any kind will do. I even use old dandelion wine that has turned to vinegar. It's a great way to get rid of old wines. And you can't taste them after the meat is cooked."

Perry Wilder, Colrain, MA

ROASTS

Roast Venison

Wash meat in vinegar and water to remove the odor. Take a tin can, coffee-sized, and wash it. Take one clove minced garlic and one chopped onion and one-half cup vinegar and one cup water. Put in the tin can and place on top of stove. When you can smell the vinegar, pour it on top of meat. Put meat in oven to roast. This way the meat is tenderized, it's sweet, and it's delicious. I roast with an oven temperature just enough to keep it warm.

Mary Garchow, Drummond Island, MI

"After selecting the roast at the market, if the rib is too long for the roast to present a symmetrical appearance, have the butcher saw off about four inches of the rib and remove the chine, leaving the ribs in the roast. All meats are better flavored and more nutritious by being cooked without removing at least some of the bones. To prepare for roasting, wash the meat and wipe dry with a towel, dredge with salt and pepper, put in the pan on a rack, if you have one, pour a pint of water in the pan and put in the oven. The oven should be very hot for the first ten to fifteen minutes to harden the albumen, after that a more moderate heat will answer. The time required to roast beef is from ten to twenty minutes to the pound, according as it is to be rare, medium or well done. Baste every ten or fifteen minutes. Some cooks dredge the roast with flour to prevent the juices from escaping. A few minutes before serving, remove the meat from the pan, place in the warming closet and into the gravy stir a tablespoonful of flour mixed with half a cup of water. If there is too much fat it should be skimmed off before thickening the gravy. Serve the roast on a hot platter and the gravy in a hot boat."

The Century Cook Book, 1894

Roast Turkey

Boil turkey until it's almost done. Next day stuff it, cover with foil, stick it in the oven and let it brown. I never cooked it any other way.

Ida Herrick, Conway, MA

To Roast a Stuffed Chicken

Build the fire *real hot*—until you can't hold your hand in the oven for very long—then put the chicken in the bottom and let the fire die slowly. It should be done in forty-five minutes to an hour.

Barbara Streeter, Madison, CT

Turkey Stuffed with Chestnuts

Put three dozen chestnuts in a pan, and bake in the oven; as the skin begins to crack take them out, skin and chop fine; put in a frying pan with a piece of butter, half an onion cut fine, and fry to a nice brown; put in a glass of port wine; mix enough soaked bread with the chestnuts to make the amount of stuffing wanted; season with salt and pepper, a little thyme; mix in four eggs and stuff turkey.

The Century Cook Book, 1894

How to Know a Young Turkey: If the lower joints of the legs are a dark red it is a young turkey. If they are white it is an old one. This is a sure sign. I never knew it to fail.

Domestic Cookery, 1888

Scotch Roll (Beef)

Take four or five pounds of the flank of a beef, wash and dry with a towel, spread on a board and dredge with salt and pepper. Make a dressing of a quart of bread crumbs, moistened with milk or water, and seasoned with two tablespoonfuls of melted butter, a small onion chopped fine, a tablespoonful of powdered sage, and pepper and salt to taste, mix all well together and spread evenly over the meat. Roll up and tie with twine, put in a pan with a pint of water and bake for two or three hours, rolling over often so as to cook even on all sides.

The Century Cook Book, 1894

Dutch Oven Roasts

Brown the roast on the bottom of the Dutch oven. Remove roast, insert the lift (or something which lifts meat off the bottom). Add one cup water, onions, and anything else you want. Cover pot and slowly cook on top of the stove until meat is cooked and tender.

Mary Garchow, Drummond Island, MI

ACCOMPANIMENTS

Grandmother's Potato Cake

"This recipe was brought from New Brunswick by my grand-mother in about the mid-1800's. It's still a wonderful dish to serve with roast beef or other meats."

Pat Scheindel, Randolph Center, VT

2 eggs, beaten
1 heaping cup mashed
  potato
1 cup milk

1½ cups flour
4 tsp. baking powder
1 tsp. salt
1 tsp. butter, melted

Add the mashed potatoes to the eggs and beat until smooth. Add the milk gradually, beating until smooth. Sift flour, baking powder, and salt; add to potatoes. Add the melted butter and beat thoroughly. Bake in two layer cake pans, greased, in a hot oven for thirty minutes. Butter each layer and serve with gravy or meat drippings.

Oven Fries

Peel and slice potatoes medium thin. Soak in cold water about thirty minutes—this removes some of the starch. Drain, and dry by dumping on paper towels. Spread potatoes on cookie sheet with sides or on a large flat pan. Sprinkle with melted oleo or butter. Place in a hot oven—about 400°F. Flip with pancake turner every ten or fifteen minutes until golden crisp on edges and soft inside. Remove to brown paper bags or paper towels. Salt well. May be kept warm in the warming oven until dinner's ready.

Barbara Streeter, Madison, CT

Creamy Broccoli Casserole

1½ lbs. broccoli
2 Tbsp. lemon juice
1 can cream of chicken
   soup
¼ cup mayonnaise

2 tsp. curry powder
1 lb. mushrooms, sliced
   and sautéed
½ cup bread crumbs
2 Tbsp. butter, melted

Cook and drain broccoli. Put on the bottom of a shallow baking dish and sprinkle with lemon juice. Mix together the soup, mayonnaise, curry powder, and mushrooms. Pour over broccoli. Cover with bread crumbs and drizzle on melted butter. Bake for twenty minutes at 350°F.

Joanne Bray, East Randolph, VT

Corn in Husks

From as many ears of corn as you plan to eat, take off a couple of layers of the husks—keeping on at least two layers to protect the kernels. The number of husks removed depends on the hotness of the oven. Bake thirty minutes to one hour. This is absolutely delicious and there are no vitamins lost.

Gladys Dimock, Bethel, VT

Pain D'Epinard

5 lbs. spinach, cleaned and
destemmed
3½ Tbsp. butter
3½ Tbsp. flour
1 cup milk

3 egg yolks
Salt, pepper, nutmeg
3½ Tbsp. Gruyere cheese,
grated

Drop the spinach into boiling salted water. When the spinach comes to a second boil, remove at once and refresh under cold water. Drain in a colander and set aside. When cool, squeeze the spinach (a small amount at a time) to extract as much water as possible. Chop the spinach a little. Make a white sauce from the butter, flour and milk. Add the egg yolks and cook for four minutes. Be sure to do this over low heat so as not to cook the yolks. Add seasonings and cheese. Incorporate the sauce into the spinach and place in a buttered mold. Set mold in a pan of hot water and bake for thirty minutes in a 375°F. oven. Unmold and spread a very thin, runny white sauce on top. Serve.

Anne Olson, Flint, MI

Make baked potatoes by oiling and pricking skins, covering them in heavy-duty foil and sticking them in the coals to cook. Takes about forty-five minutes.

Spring Favorite

Peanut oil
Young snow peas
Scallions, tops and all

Tamari sauce
Sesame seeds, toasted

Heat a wok or heavy skillet. Add oil and add as many pea pods and scallions as you feel like eating. Stir until cooked but crispy. Splash on a little tamari. Serve topped with sesame seeds.

Spring Fungus

2–3 cups morel mushrooms, sliced (or button mushrooms from store)
2–3 Tbsp. butter

¾ cup sour cream
½ cup sherry
Chopped chives

Sauté mushrooms in butter until limp. Add sour cream and sherry; heat. Pour over rice, potatoes, or enjoy them all by themselves. Top with chives.

Sesame Squash Delight   Serves 6

6 cups winter squash, peeled and cut into one-inch chunks
1 cup honey
½ cup sesame seeds, toasted

1 tsp. basil
Salt and pepper to taste
Oil
Butter

In a mixing bowl, combine squash, honey, sesame seeds, basil, salt, and pepper. Grease a large casserole with oil and put in squash mixture. Dot the top with butter and bake in a moderate oven until soft, about forty minutes.

Barbara Ernst, East Randolph, VT

Tuscan Beans

1½ cups dried white beans,   ¾ tsp. salt
   soaked overnight   ¼ tsp. freshly ground
3 Tbsp. butter   pepper
3 Tbsp. olive oil   1/3 cup canned Italian plum
1 tsp. sage   tomatoes, chopped

Drain beans and put in a Dutch oven with water to cover. Bring to a boil and move to a lower heat to simmer for about forty-five minutes, partially covered. Beans should be tender but not so they break open. Drain. In a large skillet, heat the butter and olive oil over moderate heat. Add the beans, sage, salt and pepper; cool for three minutes. Add the tomatoes; cook two or three minutes longer. Serve.

Baked Beans

"This recipe is an old Vermont family recipe, great for the old cookstove. The long cooking time brings out the most delicious flavor."

Leila MacGregor, Tunbridge, VT

2 cups dry soldier beans,   ½ cup sugar
   soaked overnight   2 tsp. salt
Small piece of salt pork   2 tsp. dry mustard
1 small onion, sliced   ¼ tsp. ginger
1/3 cup molasses   Dash of pepper

Drain beans. Put in a kettle, cover with water, and boil until tender. Pour into bean pot and add remaining ingredients. Bake in a slow oven (300°F.) for eight hours. Add water as needed and stir through.

Baked Beans with Partridge

2 cups pea beans	Salt pork (about one inch
4 Tbsp. molasses	thick and three inches
2 tsp. salt	long)
½ tsp. mustard	1 partridge ready for
2 small onions	cooking, whole

Soak beans overnight. Place in beanpot and cover with water beans were soaked in and add rest of ingredients. Place partridge in the middle of beans. Bake four to five hours at about 350°F. Add water when necessary. Don't add too much the last hour of cooking.

Carolyn T. Kelley, Camden, ME

Insalata Palermo

1 lb. young dandelion greens, preferably picked from flowerless stalks	2 eggs, beaten
	1 tsp. salt
	½ tsp. pepper
4 slices bacon, diced	½ tsp. paprika
2 Tbsp. butter, melted	1 Tbsp. honey
¼ cup thick cream, sweet or sour	1 Tbsp. cider vinegar

Wash and dry greens. Place in a salad bowl. Fry bacon until crisp, and pour bacon pieces and drippings over dandelions. Heat the butter in the same skillet; add cream, eggs, salt, pepper, paprika, honey, and vinegar. Cook over low heat, stirring constantly until mixture has thickened. Pour over dandelions; toss until thoroughly blended. Serve.

Philip Angell, Randolph Center, VT

Apple or Rhubarb Sauce

While you're preparing dinner, put a batch of sliced winter apples (McIntosh, Cortland, Rome Beauties, etc.) in a heavy earthware casserole. Sweeten with honey, and spice with whatever. Cover and stick in the oven. Bake overnight. In the morning, you should have a thick and juicy mixture, pink in color, with the apples having still retained their shape.

Gladys Dimock, Bethel, VT

Crunchy Stuffed Squash   Serves 4

2 acorn squash
¼ cup butter
1 large tart apple, diced
½ cup walnuts, chopped

Brown sugar or maple
  syrup
Cinnamon
Salt

Bake squash, uncovered and whole, in a moderate oven for about fifty minutes, or until nearly soft. Remove from oven, slice in half, and scoop out seeds. Melt butter and sauté apple until lightly browned. Fill squash cavity with apple, walnuts, sweetener, generous dashes of cinnamon, and frugal dashes of salt. Return squash to oven and bake until tender. By placing squash on the upper rack, the tops will brown nicely.

Popcorn

Popcorn pops beautifully on a wood stove. When you have a nice hot fire, just add one-half cup oil in a heavy pan. Cover and heat oil—add popcorn and shake slowly with cover on. Soon it will pop into big fluffy bits.

Carolyn T. Kelley, Camden, ME

BREADS

Zucchini Bread

4 eggs, well beaten
2 cups sugar
1 cup oil
3½ cups flour
1 tsp. salt
1½ tsp. baking soda
1 tsp. cinnamon

¾ tsp. baking powder
2 cups zucchini, grated
  and unpared
1 cup walnuts, chopped
1 cup raisins
3 tsp. vanilla

Combine eggs and sugar; add oil and beat. Combine dry ingredients and add, alternating with zucchini, to egg mixture. Stir in nuts, raisins, and vanilla. Pour into two greased loaf pans. Bake in a moderate oven for about one hour.

Gretchen Adsit, Starksboro, VT

Wholewheat Bread   Makes 2 loaves

"A lot of beginners seem to have trouble getting whole grain to rise. This recipe always works."

Barbara MacCarthy, Wileyville, WV

3 cups lukewarm water
2 or 3 Tbsp. dry yeast
¾ cup honey
¼ cup oil

5 cups wholewheat flour
¼ tsp. mace
1 Tbsp. salt
2–3 cups wholewheat flour

Combine water, yeast, and honey. Allow to soften five minutes —very important. Add oil, five cups flour, mace, and salt. Beat with an egg beater or wooden spoon five minutes. Stir in well two to three cups more flour. Knead slowly adding more flour until soft and elastic but still a little sticky. Let rise in a greased bowl, greasing bread on all sides before setting it to rise. Cover with a towel, set in the warming oven, and let rise until double in bulk. Punch down dough. Divide in half. Roll out each half with a rolling pin. Roll up jelly roll style to fit into bread pan. Set in pan with seam down; grease top of loaf. Let rise until one inch above edge of pan. Set in warm oven and bring up to a moderately-hot (375°F.) heat. Bake for forty-five minutes or until top is dark brown.

Tunbridge Cakes

Rub six ounces of butter quite fine into a pound of flour, then mix six ounces of sugar, beat and strain two eggs, and make with the above into a paste. Roll it very thin, and cut with the top of a glass, prick them with a fork, and cover with caraway, or wash with the white of an egg and dust with a little sugar over. Bake in a cool oven.

The Southern Cookbook, 1912

Potato Yeast Bread

Absolutely the lightest bread I've ever eaten! This recipe comes from a friend who has been baking bread for over forty years.

POTATO YEAST

3 medium potatoes, pared
   and diced
4 cups boiling water
1 yeast cake

1 cup sifted flour
1/3 cup sugar
1½ tsp. salt

Cook potatoes in boiling water until tender. Drain and save liquid. Cool to lukewarm. Soften yeast in one cup lukewarm potato water; add potatoes and remaining ingredients. Beat well. Cover and let stand at room temperature twenty-four hours. Pour into sterilized jar and store in a cool, dark place. Use one cup potato yeast to replace one yeast cake in any recipe. Fresh starter should be prepared at least every two weeks, using one cup of old yeast or one new cake of yeast.

BREAD

1 cup potato yeast
¼ cup lukewarm water
1 tsp. sugar
1½ tsp. salt

2 Tbsp. shortening
2 Tbsp. sugar
2 cups scalded milk
6 cups flour, sifted

Mix together potato yeast, lukewarm water, and one tsp. sugar. Let stand ten minutes. Then proceed as with any bread recipe. Bake in a moderate oven until golden brown on top.

                    Leonard Thomas, East Randolph, VT

A pan of water set on the oven floor gives bread volume and makes the temperature easier to control.

Carolyn's Health Bread　　Makes 3-4 loaves

"The more often you make the bread, the more it improves, even if you use the same recipe."

Carolyn Tonnelli-Knight, Bethel, VT

3 cups warm water
1 Tbsp. dry yeast
½ cup honey
1 cup dried milk
3-4 cups whole-wheat flour
1 Tbsp. salt
½ cup oil
½ cup soy flour
¼ cup bran
Handful of sesame seeds
½ cup wheat germ
2 Tbsp. brewer's yeast
Handful of buckwheat
　groats (optional)
Flour

Dissolve yeast in water. Add honey, dried milk, and enough flour to give mixture a muddy consistency. Set this mixture—or sponge—aside from one to four hours. This will help to give bread more lightness. Never add salt at this stage as it inhibits the rising. Later, add rest of ingredients with enough flour to give dough a kneading consistency. Proceed as you would with any bread recipe, making sure not to let the dough rise in the pans more than a half-hour; otherwise the bread will be spongy with large air holes in it.

Dingbats

After the bread dough had raised once, mom would pinch off a small bit and stretch it in a thin, flat sheet. She poked a hole in the center of the dough with her finger and laid the dough carefully into a hot greased skillet. When it was nicely brown and cooked halfway through, she turned it with a fork and cooked and browned the other side. Mom called them *fried bread,* we called them *dough-gods,* and my kids always refer to them as *ding-bats,* because of one who couldn't talk too plain.

Shirley Sweedman, Max, MN

Granola Casserole Bread

3 cups unbleached
white flour
1 package dry yeast
1¼ cups water
3 Tbsp. molasses

2 Tbsp. butter
1 tsp. salt
1 egg
1½ cups homemade granola

In a large mixing bowl, combine two cups flour and yeast. In a saucepan, heat together water, molasses, butter, and salt; stir constantly till butter almost melts. Add to dry mixture. Add egg. Beat for five minutes by hand or three minutes at high speed in an electric mixer. By hand, stir in remaining flour and granola until dough is well mixed. Place in a well-greased 1½ quart casserole, cover loosely with a damp towel and let rise in warming oven until double in bulk. Bake in a 325°F. oven for forty-five minutes; if the top starts to brown too fast, move to the bottom of the oven and cover casserole with foil. Remove bread from casserole and brush top with melted butter.

Linda Mullestein, E. Brookfield, VT

Toast

"I remember the wonderful homemade bread toasted on the stove. My mother used a long-handled rack. It was like the old type one put a steak in and held over the fire—then turned over to toast the other side. Then she'd scrape the worst burnt off (some part always burnt), butter it, and stack it in the warming oven to keep until we came down for breakfast. Bakery bread burns too easily to do it, so my mother said it could only be done with homemade bread."

Georgene Goetting, Beaver Dam, WI

Also make delicious toast by putting a slice of bread directly on top of the lids over the firebox. If it sticks when you go to turn it, wait a minute; it will lift right off.

Dill Bread

"This bread is good even if you don't let it rise twice."
Laura Sheppard, Williamstown, MA

1 package dry yeast
¼ cup warm water
1 cup large curd cottage
   cheese
2 Tbsp. butter
1 egg

1 Tbsp. onion, minced
2 tsp. dill or dill seed
1 tsp. salt
¼ tsp. baking soda
2 Tbsp. sugar
2¼-2½ cups flour, sifted

Dissolve yeast in warm water. Heat cottage cheese to luke-warm; add butter. In a large mixing bowl, combine cottage cheese mixture with all other ingredients, except flour. Mix well. Stir in a half-cup flour and beat well. Blend in enough of the remaining flour with a wooden spoon until dough leaves sides of bowl. Knead five minutes. Let rise in greased bowl until double. Punch down and let rise again. Bake in a moderate oven for forty minutes.

Brown Bread

"We've used this recipe in our family for at least four generations; in fact, it may even go further back than that."
Olive Edson, E. Randolph, VT

1 cup boiling water
1 cup Indian meal
½ cup graham flour or rye
   meal
2/3 cup molasses
1 cup sour milk
1 tsp. saleratus (baking
   soda)

½ tsp. salt
And a lot of raisins
   (raisins were a luxury,
   and such an addition
   made this real classy)
1 cup white flour

Pour the boiling water over the Indian meal. Mix in every-thing. Grease a pail or pan well, fill two-thirds full, grease cover and put it on. Set the pail or pan in a kettle of water with enough in it so pail is covered and water doesn't boil over. (They used tin lard pails or maple sugar pails, but any type, with a cover, will do. Or try using a double boiler.) Boil gently for three hours. Have to keep watching it; when it's going to storm, the water boils away faster. To test for doneness, stick a broom corn (a broom straw) into the bread: If it comes out sticky when you run your fingers down it, give bread ten to fifteen minutes more. Run a knife around the edge of the pail or pan to remove.

Potato Doughnuts

2 eggs, beaten	4½ cups flour
1 cup sugar	4 tsp. baking powder
2 Tbsp. oil	1 tsp. salt
1 cup mashed potatoes	1 tsp. soda
(or pumpkin or apples)	1 tsp. nutmeg
1 cup sour milk	

Beat eggs and sugar until light. Add oil, potato, and milk; beat until smooth. Sift flour with rest of dry ingredients. Combine with liquid ingredients. Roll half-inch thick on floured board, cut, and fry in 365°F. fat.

Bette Silloway, Randolph Center, VT

Oat Cakes

This is a specialty sold along the Cabot Trail in Nova Scotia. A friend who bicycled there swore by them during her ride.

1 cup shortening
1 cup brown sugar
¼ cup milk
1 tsp. vanilla
½ tsp. soda

½ tsp. baking powder
2 cups oatmeal
2 cups flour
1 tsp. salt

Cream shortening and sugar. Add milk and vanilla. Add dry ingredients. Roll out using oatmeal instead of flour. Cut into rounds. Bake in a moderate oven until light brown. To avoid problems with sticking, roll out between two pieces of wax paper.

Sherry Streeter

English Muffins

1 package dry yeast
2 Tbsp. warm water
1 cup hot water
½ cup milk, scalded
2 tsp. honey

4 cups unbleached white
  flour, sifted
1 tsp. salt
3 Tbsp. butter, softened

Dissolve yeast in warm water. In a mixing bowl, combine the hot water, milk, and honey. Add the yeast water and beat in two cups of the flour. Cover bowl with a damp cloth and let rise for about 1½ hours, or until dough falls back on itself. Stir in the salt and butter; knead in the remaining flour. Let rise again until doubled in bulk. Place dough on a lightly floured board, pull off enough to pat into rounds three inches across and three-quarter inches thick. Let them stand until doubled in bulk. Cook on a moderately hot, well-buttered griddle until browned on both sides, turning only once.

Graham Gems

Two cups of graham flour; one cup white flour; one teaspoonful of salt; one heaped tablespoonful of lard; two and one-half cups of warm sweet milk; three eggs beaten separately; three teaspoonfuls of baking powder; mix the graham and white flour, salt and lard together; then add the warm milk and beaten yolks; then beat the whites with two teaspoonfuls of white sugar to a stiff foam and stir them in, and last, add the baking powder. Heat the gem pans, grease them, put in the batter quickly and bake in a quick oven.

Domestic Cookery, **1888**

When making muffins, gems and cupcakes, fill one of the molds with water and there won't be a problem with burning.

As well as using the warming oven, bread can be set to rise on the warming shelves and trivets. Don't, however, set the trivets over the hot stove, as that heat would be excessive.

Corn Meal Crackers

1 cup yellow corn
  meal
½ tsp. salt, celery, onion, or
  garlic

1 Tbsp. oil
⅞ cup boiling water
¼ cup sesame or poppy
  seeds

Combine all ingredients. Drop by tablespoon on an oiled baking sheet and spread into three-inch or four-inch rounds. (The bottom of a glass works well.) Bake in a hot oven until golden. Watch carefully as these can burn easily, especially that side next to the firebox.

Bagels

4 cups unbleached white flour
2 tsp. salt
1 Tbsp. dry yeast
1 cup lukewarm water
   or potato water
2 eggs, separated

3 Tbsp. sugar
3 Tbsp. oil
3 quarts water, boiling
1 tsp. cold water
Poppy seeds, coarse salt,
   or sesame seeds

Sift 3½ cups flour and salt; save ½ cup flour for kneading. Soften yeast in half the potato water; stir into flour. Reserve one tablespoon of egg yolk and beat remaining eggs lightly. Add sugar, eggs and oil to remaining potato water and blend with flour mixture. Beat to make a dough, adding more flour, if necessary, to make it fairly stiff. Knead until smooth and elastic. Place in an oiled bowl, cover with a damp towel, and let rise until doubled in bulk. Punch and knead again until air is pressed out and dough is smooth. Pull off pieces of dough and roll into ropes about seven inches long and ¾-inch thick. Make a ring by moistening ends and squeezing slightly to seal. Let stand for ten minutes. Slide a few at a time into the boiling water, but do not overlap. Turn after one minute, cook one minute more, and remove with a slotted spoon. They will be very slippery. Mix egg yolk with the cold water and brush bagel tops with it. Place bagels on a greased cookie sheet and sprinkle with one or more of the toppings. Bake in a *hot* oven for fifteen to twenty minutes, or until golden.

Rick Yeiser, Concord, MA

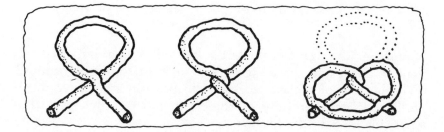

Pretzels

2 cups warm water	1 egg
2 packages dry yeast	7-7½ cups flour
½ cup sugar	1 egg yolk, beaten
2¼ tsp. salt	Coarse salt, sesame
4 Tbsp. butter, softened	seeds, or poppy seeds

Dissolve yeast in water. Add sugar, salt, butter, egg, and three cups flour. Beat to make a smooth batter—an electric mixer is a big help. Add enough flour to make a stiff dough. Cover bowl and refrigerate from four to six hours. Lightly flour a bread board. Divide dough in half; cut each half into fifteen pieces. Roll each piece between your hands so that it's eighteen inches long. Work fast because the dough is apt to shrink. Shape into pretzels and pinch the ends together. Brush the top of each generously with the egg yolk and sprinkle on one of the toppings. Arrange pretzels on a lightly greased baking sheet. Cover with a damp towel and let rise in the warming oven for thirty minutes. Bake in a moderate oven for fifteen minutes, or until golden.

Flaten Brau

My mother-in-law taught me to make this. When the dough had raised once, she would sweep out the oven very clean, then wipe it with a damp cloth. Next she would cut off a loaf sized piece of bread dough, flatten it to half an inch and lay it in the bottom of the oven to bake without first raising it. It is unbelievably heavy and delicious. If your cookstove is old and the oven is rusty, don't despair. Simply cover the bottom of the oven with a piece of foil, lay the bread dough on it and bake.

Shirley Sweedman, Max, MI.

Torta de Elote
(Fresh Corn Bread)

2 sticks butter	2 Tbsp. milk
4 eggs, separated	2 tsp. baking powder
1 cup sugar	1¾ Tbsp. rice flour
6 ears sweet corn, de-cobbed	

Cream butter and sugar; add egg yolks. Blend in corn and milk. Add baking powder and flour. Fold in stiffly beaten egg whites. Pour into a greased pan. Bake for one hour in a moderate oven.

Rebeca Median Andrade, Guadalajara, Mexico

George-Henry's Perfect
Cornbread

Sift together 1½ cups cornmeal, 1½ cups flour, one tsp. salt, three tsp. baking powder, and ¼ cup sugar. Add just enough milk to make a thick batter consistency. Add one egg, and two tsp. warm bacon fat and pour into *hot* lavishly bacon-greased pan and bake in hot oven until done, ½-¾ hour. Fry leftover pieces, split, in butter, for satisfying breakfast.

Gwen Robinson, Orford, NH

Graham Crackers

Take one part cream to four parts milk, mix with flour, as soft as can be handled, knead twenty minutes, roll very thin; cut square or round and bake quickly twenty minutes. Handle carefully while hot, pack away when cool in a stone jar.

Women's Suffrage Cook Book, 1886

Spider Marine Cake

Butter a ten-inch iron spider (skillet) and add three cups grated raw corn to the following Johnnycake recipe:

1 cup sour milk	1 tsp. soda
1 Tbsp. sour cream	1 cup flour
3 Tbsp. honey	2/3 cup Indian meal
1 tsp. salt	

Mix ingredients and pour into hot buttered skillet and top it with the grated raw corn. Bake in a 350°F. oven and test with a broom corn for doneness.

Olive Edson, East Randolph, VT

Flour Tortillas

3 cups unbleached white flour	1 tsp. salt
½ cup whole-wheat flour	1 tsp. baking powder
½ cup soya flour	1/3 cup shortening
	1 cup water

Mix flours, salt, and baking powder. Add shortening and mix well with your hands. Add water, little by little, until like a pie crust dough. Make balls, Ping Pong ball or walnut sized. Cover and let stand twenty minutes, or until ready to roll out. Roll out thin and toast on a griddle, turning when bubbles form. (If your stove top is clean, use that instead of a griddle.) Serve hot. Can be reheated to soften, or are good left in a warm place. They become crispy like crackers.

DESSERTS

CAKES

Applesauce Cake

1 cup brown sugar
¼ cup shortening
1 cup raisins, chopped
1 tsp. each, cinnamon, cloves, and nutmeg

1 cup unsweetened apple-sauce
1 tsp. soda, dissolved in a little hot water
2 cups flour
½ tsp. salt

Cream sugar and shortening. Add rest of ingredients, pour into greased pans, and bake in a moderate oven.

Grandmother Reed, Dalton, MA

Groom's Cake

One pound of white granulated sugar, ten ounces of fresh butter, sixteen yolks of fresh eggs, one pound of sifted flour, with four teaspoonfuls of baking powder mixed with it, two nutmegs grated, one gill (½ cup) of brandy, one gill of sherry wine, eight ounces of currants, weighed after they have been washed and dried. Dredge the currants with one tablespoonful of the weighed flour, warm the flour by setting the vessel containing it in hot water. Beat the butter and sugar together to a light cream, beat the yolks with a spoonful of cold milk and stir them into the butter and sugar, beat them together until very light, then add the nutmeg; then stir in the flour and baking powder. Then add the brandy and wine and last the currants; mix it well together and put it quickly into a buttered cake pan and bake one hour and twenty minutes.

Domestic Cookery, 1888

Agatha's Carrot Cake

2 cups flour	1½ tsp. vanilla
2 cups sugar	1 cup walnuts
2 tsp. baking powder	2 cups carrots, grated
2 tsp. baking soda	1 small can pineapple, with
2 tsp. cinnamon	juice
1 tsp. salt	1 recipe Pineapple
1¼ cups oil	Frosting (p. 162)
3 eggs	

Combine dry ingredients. In separate mixing bowl, combine oil, eggs, and vanilla. Gently beat in dry ingredients; add walnuts, carrots, and pineapple. Pour into a greased and dusted pan and bake in a moderate oven for one hour. Frost with Pineapple Frosting.

Agatha Youngblood, La Joya, CA

Pineapple Frosting

1 small can pineapple,
   drained
½ stick butter, softened

8 oz. cream cheese
2 tsp. vanilla
1 box confectioners' sugar

Mix everything until smooth and creamy. Spread on cooled cake. If frosting is too thick, add a little pineapple juice.

Luscious Lemon Cake

3 cups flour, sifted
½ tsp. salt
1 cup shortening
2 cups sugar
4 eggs

2 Tbsp. lemon extract
1 cup buttermilk
½ tsp. soda
½ tsp. baking powder

Sift together flour and salt into a large bowl. Add rest of ingredients. Beat for three minutes with an electric mixer. Pour into a greased tube angel food cake pan. Bake at 325°F. for one hour or until cake tester comes out clean. Frost with Luscious Lemon Glaze.

Mary Garchow, Drummond Island, MI

Luscious Lemon Glaze

5 Tbsp. lemon juice
5 Tbsp. orange juice
1-2/3 cups powdered sugar

Mix together ingredients. Pour glaze over cake while warm and return to oven for three minutes. Remove from oven. Cool before loosening edges of cake. Invert on platter, and turn right side up before slicing. Delicious, and it keeps a long time.

Nutty Tomato Cake

3 cups flour, sifted
2 tsp. baking powder
1 tsp. soda
1 tsp. nutmeg
½ tsp. salt
1 cup brown sugar
½ cup butter
2 eggs

1 16 oz. can whole
   tomatoes, blended to a
   purée
½ cup pecans or walnuts,
   chopped
½ cup dates, chopped
½ cup raisins

Sift together the flour, baking powder, soda, nutmeg, and salt. Cream brown sugar and butter; add eggs, tomatoes, nuts, dates, and raisins. Gently beat in flour mixture. Pour into a greased and dusted pan and bake one hour in a moderate oven. Use the Pineapple Frosting, with or without the pineapple.

Aunt Orlee's Pecan Date Cake

A Christmas favorite, but delectable any time of year.

1 cup flour
2 tsp. baking powder
½ tsp. salt
4 eggs, separated

1 cup sugar
1 tsp. vanilla
1 lb. pitted dates
1 lb. pecans, chopped

Sift together flour, baking powder, and salt. Cream egg yolks and sugar. Gently beat in dry ingredients. Fold in stiffly beaten egg whites. Add vanilla. Add dates and nuts, a few at a time, that have been floured. Bake at 250°F. for forty-five minutes.

Orlee Nicks, Corpus Christi, TX

To substitute honey for one cup sugar, reduce liquid by one-fourth cup and reduce baking temperature 25°.

Aunt Orlee's White Fruit Cake

¾ cup butter
2 cups sugar
2 cups flour
2 tsp. baking powder
6 eggs, separated
½ cup bourbon

1 nutmeg, grated
1 lb. pecans
1 lb. cherries
1 lb. pineapple
½ cup grated coconut

Cream butter and sugar. Sift together flour and baking powder. Stir in egg yolks and bourbon. Gently beat in dry ingredients. Fold in stiffly beaten egg whites. Add nutmeg, cherries, pineapple, and coconut. Bake at 250°F. for two hours.

Orlee Nicks, Corpus Christi, TX

Doctor's Cake

One pint of sweet milk, two ounces of fresh butter, one teaspoonful of grated nutmeg, one teaspoonful of salt, half a pint of white granulated sugar, four fresh eggs beaten separately, one quart of flour, four teaspoonfuls of Royal baking powder. Put the milk, butter, nutmeg, salt, and sugar into a saucepan over the fire, and when the butter is melted and sugar dissolved, set it on the side of the range where it will keep warm, but not hot. Beat the yolks and stir them into the milk, beat the whites with one tablespoonful of white sugar to a stiff foam, mix the flour and baking powder together. Stir the milk into the flour until it is as thick as batter cakes, then stir in the whites and the rest of the flour.

Domestic Cookery, 1888

COOKIES

Frosted Carrot Bars

4 eggs
2 cups sugar
2 cups flour, sifted
2 tsp. baking powder
2 tsp. cinnamon
1 tsp. salt

1½ cups oil
3 cups carrots, finely
  grated
1½ cups grated coconut
1½ cups walnuts, chopped

Beat the eggs until light and gradually add the sugar. Sift together the flour, baking powder, cinnamon, and salt. Add flour mixture to egg mixture alternately with oil. Fold in the carrots, coconut, and walnuts. Spread mixture in two greased 13 x 9 x 2-inch pans. Bake at 350°F. for twenty-five to thirty minutes. Cool and frost with Cream Cheese Frosting.

Cream Cheese Frosting

3 oz. cream cheese
1 Tbsp. light cream
2½ cups confectioner's
  sugar

1 tsp. vanilla
⅛ tsp. salt

Blend together the cream cheese and cream. Add the sugar and more cream, if necessary, to make frosting spreadable. Add vanilla and salt and beat well.

Joanne Bray, East Randolph, VT

10/07 =

Apple-Oatmeal Chews

1 cup whole-wheat flour, sifted	2/3 cup brown sugar
½ tsp. baking soda	½ cup melted shortening *> Butter*
½ tsp. salt	1 egg
1 tsp. cinnamon	¼ tsp. vanilla *½ tsp*
⅛ tsp. allspice	2 cups apples, pared *2 apples*
1 tsp. grated orange rind *(omit)*	and thinly sliced
1-1/3 cups uncooked oatmeal *used 5 grams*	Confectioners' sugar *(omit)*

Sift together flour, baking soda, salt, cinnamon, and allspice. Add remaining ingredients, except apples and confectioners' sugar. Knead with hands to mix well. Pat half the dough over the bottom of a greased 9 x 9 x 2-inch baking pan. Arrange apples evenly on top. Pat on rest of dough. Bake in a moderate oven for about thirty minutes, or until top begins to pull from sides of pan. Cool until warm to the touch and press top layer firmly into apples. Dust with sugar, cool to room temperature, and cut into squares.

T.J. Goetting, Odessa, MD

Date Bars

1 cup honey or maple syrup	2 eggs
1 cup flour	1 tsp. vanilla
1 cup dates, chopped	1 tsp. baking powder
1 cup nutmeats, chopped	¼ tsp. allspice

Mix everything together. Pour into a greased baking pan. Bake for thirty to forty minutes in a moderate oven. Cut into bars when cool.

Toffy Bars

Bottom layer: ½ cup butter
                ½ cup brown sugar
                1 cup flour

Cream butter and sugar; add flour. Spread in ungreased 9 x 9-inch pan. Bake for ten minutes in a moderate oven. Cool slightly.

Top layer:
2 eggs, well beaten   ¼ tsp. salt
1 cup brown sugar   1 cup shredded coconut
1 tsp. vanilla   1 cup pecans or walnuts,
2 Tbsp. flour   chopped
1 tsp. baking powder

Mix together everything in order. Spread over the bottom layer. Bake in a moderate oven for twenty to twenty-five minutes.

Grandmother Reed, Dalton, MA

Lacy Granola Drops

1 cup brown sugar   ½ tsp. salt
1 stick butter   1¼ cups granola
2 eggs   1 cup raisins, or currants,
1 tsp. vanilla   or chopped dates (what-
1 Tbsp. milk   ever the granola doesn't
1 cup whole-wheat flour,   have)
  sifted

Cream sugar and butter. Stir in eggs, vanilla, and milk until mixture is smooth. Add flour, salt, and granola; beat well. Stir in dried fruit. Drop by rounded tablespoon onto a greased cookie sheet. Bake for twelve minutes, or until golden, in a moderate oven.

Chocolate Macaroons

Two ounces of chocolate scraped up very fine, two ounces of sweet almonds blanched and pounded very fine, with two tea-spoonfuls of sweet milk, four ounces of white granulated sugar, one white of an egg, one teaspoonful of cornstarch, one tea-spoonful of vanilla extract, half a teaspoonful of cinnamon. Mix the chocolate and almonds well together, then stir in the sugar and beat the white with a teaspoonful of sugar to a stiff foam and stir it in, then add the vanilla and cinnamon and stir in the dry cornstarch. Cover the bottom of a baking pan with white paper and then butter it. Then put on the paper half a teaspoonful of the mixture one inch apart and put them into a slow oven and bake three-quarters of an hour or until they are hard and dry.

Domestic Cookery, **1888**

> To keep cookies from burning on bottom, turn the baking pan upside down and bake on the bottom of the pan.

Benne Seed Wafers

1¼ cups flour, sifted
¾ tsp. baking powder
½ tsp. salt
¾ cup butter, softened
1½ cups brown sugar

2 eggs
2 tsp. vanilla or 1 tsp. lemon extract
¾ cup benne seeds (sesame seeds), toasted

Sift together flour, baking powder, and salt. Cream butte and sugar; add eggs and flavoring. Stir in dry ingredients and benne seeds. Drop by rounded teaspoon onto greased cookie sheet. Bake in a moderately slow oven for ten to fifteen minutes, or until lightly browned.

Iron Delights

3½ cups whole-wheat pastry flour, sifted	½ tsp. cloves
1 tsp. baking powder	¾ cup oil
1 tsp. soda	½ cup blackstrap molasses
1 tsp. salt	¾ cup honey
2 tsp. cinnamon	1 egg
1 tsp. ginger	¾ cup yogurt
	1 cup raisins

Sift together flour, baking powder, soda, salt, cinnamon, ginger, and cloves. Mix together oil, molasses, honey, and egg. Stir in yogurt. Gently stir in dry ingredients. Drop by teaspoon onto greased cookie sheet. Bake in 375°F. oven until done.

Thurmond Knight, Bethel, VT

PIES

Basic Fruit Pie

2 Tbsp. cornstarch	1½ Tbsp. lemon juice
¼ cup water or fruit juice	Spices to taste
Sweetening to taste	2 Tbsp. butter
4 cups fresh fruit	Prepared pie crust

Mix together the cornstarch, water, and sweetener; pour over fruit. Let stand at least fifteen minutes. Gently stir in lemon juice and spices. Pour fruit mixture into pie shell, dot with butter, and cover pie with top crust.

Schloss Herblinger Apple Pie

¼ cup butter
1½ cups flour, sifted
3 Tbsp. cold water
1 Tbsp. toasted almonds, crushed
1 Tbsp. dry bread crumbs, ground

4 cups tart apples, thinly sliced
2 eggs
2 egg yolks
2 cups heavy cream
¾ cup sugar
2 Tbsp. butter, melted

Cut butter into flour with pastry blender or fingers. Add cold water gradually, mixing with fork, until pastry gathers around fork. Roll out to a thickness of one-eighth inch. Line a deep dish pie pan with pastry and trim edges. Sprinkle almonds and bread crumbs over pastry bottom. Arrange apples evenly over those. Bake in a moderate oven five minutes and remove. Combine eggs and yolks and beat slightly. Add cream and a half-cup sugar; beat. Pour half of this mixture over apples and bake until firm, about thirty minutes. Remove pie; pour melted butter evenly over top and sprinkle with remaining sugar. Return to oven for five minutes, or until top is crusty and golden.

Norma Coulter, Drummond Island, MI

"Fruit pies are the best in a wood stove. If you have no thermometer on it—just build the fire real hot, till it's mighty uncomfortable to put your hand in the oven to test it. Then *quick* put the pie in the bottom and let the fire die out slowly. After forty-five minutes, it should be done. If juice runs over onto the oven, shake some salt onto it and it will burn to a crisp and will easily brush away."

Barbara Streeter, Madison, CT

Maple-Pumpkin Pie

3 eggs, slightly beaten
½ cup brown sugar
½ cup maple syrup
½ tsp. cinnamon
½ tsp. ginger
½ tsp. salt

3 cups pumpkin, canned or cooked
1 cup cream
1 9-inch pie shell, unbaked
½ cup walnuts

Combine eggs, sugar, syrup, spices, salt, pumpkin, and cream. Beat by hand or electric mixer until smooth. Pour filling into pie shell and bake in a moderate oven until filling has set. Serve warm or cold; decorate with walnuts.

Luscious Lemon Pie

"My grandmother gave me this recipe. It's real old, but it's still the smoothest pie you'll ever eat."
Mary Garchow, Drummond Island, MI

1 cup sugar
3 Tbsp. cornstarch
1 Tbsp. butter
3 egg yolks, slightly beaten

1 lemon, juice and grated rind
1 cup milk
1 cup sour cream
1 9-inch baked pie shell

In a saucepan, mix together everything except the sour cream. Over medium-low heat, cook, stirring all the time until thick. Don't let it get lumpy. Take off stove and fold in sour cream until it melts into mixture. Pour into pie shell. Chill. Serve with whipped cream.

Boiled Cider Pie

1 cup brown or maple sugar
4 Tbsp. flour
1 egg
2 Tbsp. vinegar
6 Tbsp. boiled cider (see
    recipe pg. 184)

Butter the size of a walnut
½ tsp. nutmeg
9-inch unbaked pie crust,
    top and bottom

Beat together the sugar, flour, egg, and vinegar. Add boiled cider, butter, and nutmeg. Bake between two pie crusts till thick.

Louise Silloway, Randolph Center, VT

Fruit Crumble

4 cups fresh fruit, sliced
Cinnamon
1 cup flour, wheat germ,
    or oatmeal

2/3 cup brown sugar
1 8 oz. package cream
    cheese

Place fruit in a shallow baking pan and sprinkle with cinnamon. Mix flour, sugar, and cream cheese together coarsely, as for pie crust. Spread over fruit and bake in a moderate oven until crisp and brown. Serve with cream, ice cream, or whipped cream.

Chocolate Cheesecake

Crust:
3 Tbsp. brown sugar   1½ cups vanilla wafer or
½ stick butter, melted   graham cracker crumbs

Add sugar to crumbs and stir in melted butter. Press into and up the sides of an eight-inch spring form pan. Set aside.

Filling:
3 8 oz. packages cream   2 tsp. vanilla
  cheese, softened   3 eggs
¾ cup honey   ½ cup heavy cream
1/3 cup cocoa

Beat cream cheese until smooth. Add honey, cocoa, and vanilla. Beat in eggs and mix well. Beat in cream. Pour filling into crust and bake in a moderate oven for about forty-five minutes, or until top has browned. Cool and refrigerate at least four hours.

PUDDINGS
AND CUSTARDS

Baked Indian Pudding

Heat four cups milk in double boiler. Mix ½ cup corn meal, 2/3 cup molasses, one tsp. salt, one tsp. ginger, and a little butter. Add to hot milk and cook twenty minutes until thick. Pour into greased baking dish and pour over one cup cold milk. Do not stir. Bake in 300°F. oven two hours or more. Serve with cream.

Grandmother Reed, Dalton, MA

Plum Pudding

6 oz. suet, chopped fine
6 oz. raisins
8 oz. currants

3 oz. bread crumbs
3 oz. flour
3 eggs

One-sixth of a nutmeg; small blade of mace and cinnamon; one-half teaspoon salt; one-half pint milk (or less); four ounces sugar; one ounce candied lemon; one-half ounce candied citron.

Beat the eggs and spices well together; mix in the flour, then the rest of the ingredients. Dip a fine close linen cloth into boiling water and put it in a hair sieve. Flour it a little, pour in the mixture and tie it up close; put it into a saucepan containing six quarts of boiling water; keep a kettle of boiling water along side of it, and fill up your pot as it wastes. Be sure to keep it boiling six hours at least.

Mrs. Hale's New Cookbook, 1873

Lemon Pudding Sauce

One cup sugar, two cups water; boil about ten minutes; stir in while boiling three teaspoons cornstarch mixed up with a little cold water. Add to this the juice and grated rind of one lemon, one tablespoon butter, a pinch of salt.

The Home Queen Cookbook, 1898

Burnt Cream Sauce

Put two ounces sugar in a stew-pan over the fire. Stir till brown, then pour in slowly one gill thin cream, stirring all the time.

The Home Queen Cookbook, 1898

English Plum Pudding   Serves 16

1 cup flour
1 tsp. soda
1 tsp. salt
1 tsp. cinnamon
¼ tsp. nutmeg
¾ tsp. mace
1½ cups raisins, finely cut
1½ cups currants, plumped
¾ cup citron, finely cut
¼ cup walnuts
½ cup dates

½ cup almonds
½ cup pecans
1½ cups coarse soft bread
   crumbs
2 cups (½ lb.) ground suet
1 cup brown sugar
3 eggs, beaten
6 Tbsp. currant jelly
¼ cup fruit juice
Brandy or sherry

Sift together flour, soda, salt, and spices. Mix in following ingredients through bread crumbs. In a separate bowl, mix together remaining ingredients and blend into flour-fruit mixture. Pour into well-greased two-quart mold, or 2 one-quart molds. Steam six to twelve hours. Serve with hard sauce.

Pat Scheindel, Randolph Center, VT

Apple or Peach Pudding

2 eggs, slightly beaten
1 cup molasses or honey
3 Tbsp. wholewheat flour or
   1 tsp. cornstarch
1 tsp. baking powder

¼ tsp. salt
½ cup raisins or nuts
2 cups fresh apples or
   peaches, sliced

Combine eggs and sweetener. Add enough water to the flour or cornstarch to form a smooth paste; add to egg mixture. Stir in baking powder, salt, raisins or nuts, and fruit. Spread mixture in a buttered 9-inch pie pan or cast-iron skillet. Bake until brown and crusty at 350°F.

Barbara MacCarthy, Wileyville, WV

Rebeca's Delicious Flan

6 eggs
2 cups milk

2 cans sweetened
condensed milk

Combine ingredients and stir very well—a blender is just the thing. Bake it "al bano Maria" (by setting custard dish in a pan of hot water) in a moderate oven until custard sets.

Rebeca Median Andrade, Guadalajara, Mexico

Orange Custard

Boil very tender the rind of one-half a Seville orange; beat it in a mortar to a paste; put to it a spoonful of the best brandy, the juice of one orange, four ounces of lump-sugar, and the yolks of four eggs. Beat all together ten minutes and pour in by degrees a pint of boiling cream. Keep beating until the mixture is cold; put into custard cups and set in a soup dish of boiling water; let them stand until thick. Serve with preserved orange-peel, in slices, upon the custard. Hot or cold.

Mrs. Hale's New Cookbook, 1873

Pineapple Tapioca

4 Tbsp. tapioca
½ cup water

1 pint pineapple, chopped
Brown sugar to taste

Soak tapioca overnight. Add a half-cup water and cook over medium heat until clear. Then add pineapple and sweetener. Cook until thick.

Ida Herrick, Conway, MA

Puddings can be boiled in cloths or into buttered molds tied in cloths.

Mrs. Hale's New Cookbook, 1873

Crunchy Chocolate Custard

¼ cup walnuts or pecans,
   chopped
¼ cup macaroon pieces or
   shredded coconut
3 eggs, slightly beaten
2 Tbsp. honey

2 cups very rich chocolate
   milk, scalded
⅛ tsp. salt
½ tsp. almond extract
½ tsp. vanilla

Combine nuts and macaroons or coconut. Place one table-spoon of this in bottom of six custard cups. Combine eggs and honey; add chocolate milk and salt slowly to egg mixture. Add flavorings. Pour into custard cups. Place in a pan of hot water. Bake at 325°F. for twenty-five to thirty minutes, or until custard sets.

Caramel Custard

Put a can of sweetened condensed milk in a sauce pan and cover with water. Bring water to a boil and cook for 3½ hours. As the water evaporates, add more. Remove pan from stove and let water cool to room temperature, leaving can in the pot. Remove can and chill. Either cut off slices or spoon out custard. As this is shamelessly rich, serve small portions. Whipped cream dabbed on top makes it even more irresistible.

Peppermint Drops

Pound and sift four ounces of double refined sugar, beat it with the whites of two eggs till smooth, add sixty drops of oil of peppermint, beat it well and drop on white paper, and dry at a distance from the fire.

The Southern Cook Book, 1912

DAIRY

Cottage Cheese

"Place sour milk in a gallon jar with a tight-fitting lid. Immerse in reservoir for several hours. Place clean cloth in colander and pour heated curds from jar into colander. Allow to drain well. Empty curds into a bowl, break up with a fork, salt and pepper, moisten with sweet cream and chill. Delicious cottage cheese."

Shirley Sweedman, Max, MN

Cottage Cheese from Sour Milk

Certified raw milk

Sour milk by setting it in a heavy enamel or crockery pot and set on the back of the stove, where it is coolest, or put milk in a bowl and let stand in the warming oven. The milk should be soured in twenty-four hours. Heat the soured milk until it reaches 110°F. on a milk thermometer. When the milk has curdled, pour into a double thickness cheese cloth bag which has been set over a strainer in a bowl and drain. The ends of the cheese cloth can be tied together and the whole bundle hung from the faucet: the longer the cottage cheese drains, the thicker the product. Place cottage cheese in a bowl and season with salt and cream or yogurt. Use whatever herbs you like. The whey, or liquid which has drained from the curds, can be mixed with fruit juices for a healthy drink or is good used in bread or biscuit recipes.

Cottage Cheese with Rennet

2 quarts milk
1 junket tablet
1 Tbsp. warm water

Heat milk to 90°F. Dissolve junket tablet in water and stir into milk. Cover bowl and let stand in warming oven or on the back of the stove (if stove feels very warm, set bowl on a trivet) for about eight hours or overnight. Cut through the curd with a silver knife several times. Place bowl in a large pan of hot water and bring curd to 110°F. for soft cheese and 118°F. for farmer-style cheese. Stir curd a few times while heating. Pour curds into a double thickness cheese cloth bag and drain off whey. Place cottage cheese in a bowl and season with salt, cream, sour cream, or yogurt.

Wine Cottage Cheese

Put two quarts of rich sour unskimmed milk with half a pint of sherry wine into a porcelain saucepan, cover it and set it where it will be quite warm, but not scalding hot. When the curd has formed put it all into a linen cloth, hang it up, and when the whey has run out put the curd into a bowl with one gill of thick sweet cream and rub it together with the back of the spoon against the bowl until it is very fine, then put in two even tablespoonfuls of white granulated sugar and serve with sweetened cream. Cottage cheese made by this receipt is very fine; the wine gives it a delicious flavor, and the whey with the addition of a little more wine and sugar makes a fine healthy drink.

Mrs. Hale's New Cookbook, 1873

Yogurt

1 quart fresh milk
¼ cup dried milk
2 tsp. plain yogurt

Scald the milk. Remove from heat and stir in (or use a blender) dried milk. Cool to 110°F.—it will feel lukewarm—and stir in yogurt. The better mixed it is, the smoother the yogurt. Pour into a very clean quart jar, cover, and let stand in a warm, tranquil place for four to eight hours. (The yogurt should not be moved or jarred during incubation or it might get lumpy.) The longer the yogurt stands, the tarter it becomes. If using the warming oven, be sure to open the door as the temperature may be too great and kill the yogurt bacteria; if the oven is too cool, they will not grow.

For a sweet, custard-like yogurt, add one teaspoon vanilla, or other flavoring, and a couple tablespoons maple syrup or honey to the milk. Topped with fruit, it's a wonderful dessert.

Egg Nog, Warm

One quart of rich sweet milk, half a pint of brandy or whiskey, six ounces of white granulated sugar, one teaspoonful of grated nutmeg, three fresh eggs, beaten separately. Put the milk, brandy, sugar and nutmeg into a saucepan and set it on the side of the range, where it will get warm but not hot. Beat the whites to a stiff foam then beat the yolks and stir them into the whites, then stir them into the warm milk and sit over a quick fire, stir it fast and as soon as it begins to rise (it must not boil) take it off the fire and pour it into a bowl or pitcher and serve it in glasses. It is a very refreshing drink on a cold day.

Domestic Cookery, 1888

Cream Cheese

  4 cups sour cream
½ rennet tablet
½ tsp. salt

Put sour cream in a one-quart saucepan, either glass or stainless steel. Crush rennet tablet and mix with two tablespoons water. Stir rennet solution into cream and mix thoroughly. Place saucepan on the far end of stove (may have to set on a trivet) and *slowly* heat to 100°F. Hold it at this heat for twenty minutes; move the pan accordingly to maintain this temperature. Remove pan from heat and let cool to room temperature. Spoon cream into a double thick cheesecloth bag; hang from the kitchen faucet to drain. When cheese is drained and firm, mix in salt, form cheese into a bar, wrap in wax paper, and refrigerate.

PRESERVES

CANNING AND PICKLING

"I have almost given up making such items as tomato pre-
serves, mincemeat, chili sauce and ketchup because it is almost impossible to do a decent job of cooking these products
on any but a wood cookstove. Until necessity forced me to give
up mine, I made quarts and quarts of all of these from our
own home grown vegetables and fruit. The heavy cast iron
bottom of my twenty-one quart canner filled to the brim would
simmer half a day at a time on the back of the stove to the
proper thickness with only an occasional stir, without
scorching."

Shirley Sweedman, Max, MN

Green Tomato Mincemeat

"A good way to use all those green tomatoes when frost is imminent."

Helen Short, E. Berkshire, VT

6 lbs. green tomatoes, washed
6 lbs. apples
6 lbs. raisins
1 lb. suet, ground (optional)

1½ Tbsp. sea salt
6 tsp. cinnamon
3 tsp. cloves
3 tsp. nutmeg
1½ cups lemon juice
3 lbs. brown sugar

Cut up tomatoes and put through food grinder. Quarter and core apples and grind. Place tomatoes and apples in huge kettle with other ingredients. Cook until thick. Place in jars and seal in hot water bath. Makes seven quarts.

Boiled Cider Mincemeat

2 pints cooked meat, through meat chopper (can use tougher parts of beef or venison)
4 pints apples, cored and chopped
1 pint meat juice
1 cup cider
1 cup raisins

1½ cups sugar—with some maple syrup
1 cup molasses
1 cup ground suet
1 cup boiled cider
1 tsp. each salt, cloves, allspice, ginger, nutmeg
1/3 tsp. pepper
Citron or candied peels, if desired

Mix everything in a large, heavy pan. Simmer slowly several hours or longer until thick. Can in jars, sealing while hot. May add more apple to warm mincemeat when making pies.

Helen Boudro, Randolph Center, VT

Boiled Cider

Start with at least one gallon of cider and put in a large, wide pan. Simmer slowly until reduced to about one quart, which may take up to twenty-four hours. The consistency should be thick, almost jelly-like. However, by boiling a shorter time, you can make it like syrup. This can be used to reconstitute with water to make a refreshing drink; the thicker cider is used in cooking. Seal cider in jelly jars; it keeps very well.

Tomato Sauce

Core and cut out bad spots from a load of tomatoes. Cut each into about eight pieces. Put tomatoes into a ceramic or other heavy pot (nothing aluminum), and cook over low heat for about two days. Add whatever spices you want halfway through the cooking. Pour into jars and seal in hot water bath.

Victoria Weber, Bethel, VT

Tomato Catsup (Excellent)

Boil one bushel of tomatoes until they are soft; squeeze them through a fine wire sieve, and add half a gallon of vinegar; one and one-half pint of salt; two ounces of cloves; one-quarter pound of allspice; three ounces of cayenne pepper; three tablespoons of black pepper; five heads of garlic, skinned and separated.

Mix these together and boil about three hours, or until reduced one half. Then bottle without straining. If you want half the quantity, take half of the above.

Mrs. Hale's New Cookbook, 1873

Aunt Sarah's Chili Sauce

At least 150 years old.

4 quarts tomatoes, cut into
  quarters
2 cups onions, sliced
2 cups green peppers,
  sliced
1 Tbsp. salt
3 Tbsp. mixed pickling
  spices

1 Tbsp. mustard seed
1 Tbsp. celery seed
2½ cups cider vinegar
1 cup sugar—maple,
  brown, honey, what-
  ever (they used anything
  they had on hand)

Mix everything together in a big pot and put on back of stove so that it simmers gently for days. It's ready when it reaches the thickness you want. I like it when it kind of mounds up on your spoon. I think it also reaches its peak of flavor then.

Olive Edson, East Randolph, VT

Canned Grapes

Put washed green or blue grapes into clean jars, cover with hot sugar syrup, adjust lids accordingly to manufacturer's instructions. Place jars in reservoir of hot water until the contents are bubbly hot. Remove from water and cool as usual.

Shirley Sweedman, Max, MN

Pepper Vinegar

6 hot peppers,
  the hotter the better
1½ quarts white vinegar

Slit peppers and boil with vinegar until reduced to one quart of vinegar. Strain and bottle. This will keep for years. If very strong tasting, add more vinegar.

Peach Catsup

1 quart peaches, skinned
   and chopped
1 onion, chopped
1 cup honey
½ cup vinegar

¼ tsp. salt
½ tsp. ginger
½ tsp. cloves
½ tsp. cinnamon

Combine everything in a heavy pan. Simmer for a couple of hours, or until it reaches the thickness you want. Bottle.

Pear Relish

1 peck pears
6 large onions
4 red bell peppers

2 lbs. sugar
1 Tbsp. allspice
5 cups vinegar

Grind up pears and vegetables in food chopper. Add vinegar, sugar, and spices. Slowly cook until thick, stirring occasionally. Pour into jars and process ten minutes in boiling water bath.

DRYING

Parched Corn

"It's really delicious, but it gums up your teeth."
Victoria Weber, Bethel, VT

Overgrown sweet corn, as
    many ears as you want
Boiling water

Boil corn in water for fifteen minutes. Cut kernels off cob.
Spread kernels on a baking sheet and place in a 250°-300°F.
oven for twelve hours. This should be stirred every half hour or
so. Don't forget it, or it burns! Salt if you want to, but I like it
all by itself.

Dried Citrus Peel

Keep a jar in the warming oven to hold the grated rinds of unsprayed citrus fruits. When they have dried, store in tightly capped bottles. Great for adding to baked goods.

Dried Herbs

Gather herbs just before the plant flowers, while the leaves are still tender and green. Tie the stems in a bundle, enclose plants in a paper bag, and hang upside-down near the stove to dry. Don't let temperature exceed 100°F., though, as the flavor resides in the oils which dry out with excessive heat. And if you're drying several different kinds, label the bags. Once the herbs have dried, rub the bag between your hands to crumble the leaves from the stems. Bottle.

Apple Rings

Peel, core, and thinly slice crisp winter apples. Dip into cold salt water (four tablespoons to a gallon of water) and either arrange on a drying rack to be put in the oven (do not let temperature exceed 150°F.) or string on a thread and hang above the stove. When apples are rubbery with no trace of moisture, they've finished drying. A special treat for dieters.

Dried Onions

Onions are one vegetable that require no blanching or special preparation before drying. Select large, perfect ones. Cut off the stems and bottoms and slice thinly or chop very fine. Separate the slices into rings. Arrange onion pieces on a cookie sheet or plate and place in the oven or warming oven, watching the temperature so that it doesn't exceed 150°F. They're ready when brittle.

Mushroom Powder

Peel large, fleshy button mushrooms and cut off the stems; spread them on plates, and dry them in a slow oven. When thoroughly dry, pound them with a little cayenne and mace; bottle and keep the powder in a dry place. A teaspoonful of this powder will give the mushroom flavor to a tureen of soup, or to sauce for poultry, hashes, etc.

Mrs. Hale's New Recipe Book, 1873

Orange Chips

Cut oranges in halves, squeeze the juice through the sieve, soak the peel in water; next day boil in the same till tender, drain them, and slice the peels, put them to the juice, weigh as much sugar, and put all together into a broad earthen dish, and put over the fire at a moderate distance, often stirring until the chips candy, then set them in a cool room to dry. They will not be so under three weeks.

The Southern Cookbook, 1912

Fruit Leather

Peel, core, and cut up one pound or more of fruit—apples, peaches, apricots, pears, plums, rose hips. Place in a large pot and add one tablespoon honey for each pound of fruit. Cook until thick and mushy; if fruit becomes too dry, add a little water. Spread very thinly onto plates or a cookie sheet and place in a very slow oven or the warming oven to dry. Cut into jar-length strips, string on a line hung near the stove, and let dry twenty-four hours more. The drier they are, the longer they'll keep. Store in jars. This is a terrific snack.

HOMEMADE SOAP
AND OTHER SUNDRIES

Lye and grease are the two basic ingredients in the manu-
facture of soap. The simplest and most dependable method is
to use commercial lye: the lye is always the same strength
and the recipe measurements are exact. Lye which is leached
from wood ashes (potash) is dependent on the kind of wood
burned—hardwoods producing the strongest and most desirable lye—thus making precise proportions more difficult. But
our forefathers didn't rely on store-bought goods to meet their
needs, and if you're game, you needn't either.

To make a liquid soap for washing dishes: mix scraps of old
soap bars with water in a tin can and place on the back of the
stove. When soap melts, pour into a bottle and keep by the sink.

Potash Lye

Early New England settlers leached ashes through large wooden barrels or specially-built ash pits, but since they usually made soap in quantities to last a year, the following method is handier for experimentation on a much smaller scale.

Fill a porcelain-covered or plastic pail with wood ashes. Add boiling water (soft or medium-hard water are best for soap making) and stir so that ashes are thoroughly moistened. Fill pail with more ashes to reach the top, stir again, and let stand twelve to twenty-four hours, or until the liquid clears. Siphon or dip off the clear liquid from the top. This is the lye. The lye is of a proper strength if an egg floated in it raises partway out of the solution, forming an oval slightly more than one inch long at the solution's surface. If the lye is weak, pour it through a new pail of ashes or concentrate it by boiling. Lye is a corrosive poison and can cause serious burns: do not let it touch your skin, and if any is swallowed, take as much vinegar, citrus juice or rhubarb as possible and call a doctor. To protect yourself, work with rubber gloves and protective glasses.

Soft Soap   (Makes one cup)

½ cup potash lye
1 cup clarified fat
  or vegetable oil

Put the lye in an iron, stainless steel or ceramic kettle (never aluminum—lye will destroy it). Add the fat or oil and boil until the mixture becomes thick, rubbery, and foamy. Remove the kettle from the fire and let cool. The soap will be thick and jelly-like, ranging in color from light to dark brown, depending on the kind of fat or oil used and the amount of time it took to boil. Store soap in an iron, glass, ceramic, or wooden container for at least a month before using. To use, mix with water to work up a lather.

Fix-it Cement

2 parts wood ash
1 part clean, dry sand

3 parts powdered clay
Linseed oil

Mix together ashes, sand, and clay with enough linseed oil to form a paste. Use this for minor repairs; it's long-lasting and water-proof.

Wood Stove Cement

1 part sifted wood ash
  Water

1 part plain (not iodized)
  salt

Mix together ashes and salt with enough water to form a paste. Apply to a cool stove to fill minor cracks or seal loose joints. This is not as durable as the commercial kind, but in a pinch, it's better than nothing.

Stove Blacking

1 part powdered graphite
2 parts boiled linseed oil

Mix together ingredients and brush blacking on the stove. Keep this well stirred as the graphite prefers to settle to the bottom. Build a small fire to hasten the drying; it may take a day or so.

BIBLIOGRAPHY

Beecher, Catherine E. *Miss Beecher's Domestic Receipt Book,* New York: Harper & Brothers, 1846.

Beecher, Catherine E. *Miss Beecher's Housekeeper and Healthkeeper.* New York: Harper & Brothers, 1874.

Bivins, S. Thomas. *The Southern Cook Book.* Hampton,, VA: Press of the Hampton Institute, 1912.

Burr, Hattie A. *The Women's Suffrage Cook Book.* Boston: Festival Bazaar, 1886.

Coleman, Peter. *Wood Stove Know-How.* Pownal, VT: Garden Way Publishing, 1974.

Farmer, Fannie Merritt. *The Original Boston Cooking-School Cook Book: A Facsimile.* New York: Hugh Lauter Levin Associates, 1973.

Gay, Larry. *Heating With Wood,* Pownal, VT: Garden Way Publishing, 1974.

Hale, Mrs. *Mrs. Hale's New Cook Book.* Philadelphia: T.B. Peterson & Brothers, 1873.

Hansey, Jennie A. *The Century Cookbook.* 1894.

Hertzber, Vaughan & Greene. *Putting Food By.* Brattleboro, VT: Stephen Greene Press, 1973.

Hobson, Phyllis. *Making Soaps & Candles.* Pownal, VT: Garden Way Publishing, 1974.

Home Comfort Cook Book. Revised edition. St. Louis: Wrought Iron Range Company.

Leslie, Miss. *Miss Leslie's New Receipts for Cooking.* Philadelphia: T.B. Peterson & Brothers, 1874.

Loveday, Evelyn V. *Home Storage of Vegetables & Fruits.* Pownal, VT: Garden Way Publishing, 1972.

Pierce, Josephine H. *Fire on the Hearth.* Springfield, MA: Pond-Ekberg, 1951

Phipps, Frances. *Colonial Kitchens: Their Furnishings & Their Gardens.* New York: Hawthorne Books, 1972.

Pulte, Dr. J. H. *Domestic Cook Book.* Cincinnati: George W. Smith, 1888.

Smallzried, Kathleen Ann. *The Everlasting Pleasure: Influences on America's Kitchens, Cooks & Cookery from 1565 to the Year 2000.* New York: Appleton-Century-Crofts, Inc., 1956.

The American Heritage Cookbook & Illustrated History of American Eating and Drinking. American Heritage Publishing Co., 1964.

Using Coal and Wood Safely. Boston: National Fire Protection Association, 1974.

Wright, Lawrence. *Home Fires Burning: The History of Domestic Heating and Cooking.* London: Hillary, 1964.

INDEX